THE SURVEY OF ACADEMIC LIBRARY CATALOGING PRACTICES, 2011-12 Edition

ISBN 1-57440-178-5

Library of Congress Control Number: 2011936694

TABLE OF CONTENTS

TABLE OF CONTENTS 2
LIST OF TABLES 3
SURVEY PARTICIPANTS 28
CHARACTERISTICS OF THE SAMPLE 30
SUMMARY OF MAIN FINDINGS..31
1. Personnel Issues 46
2. Salary Issues..79
3. Work Rate Compensation 80
4. Technology 96
5. Outsourcing...101
6. State of Cataloging Education in Library Schools 121

LIST OF TABLES

Table 1.1:   Is Original Cataloging routinely done by Paraprofessional Support Staff?..............54
Table 1.2:   Is Original Cataloging routinely done by Paraprofessional Support Staff? Broken Out by FTE Student Enrollment 54
Table 1.3:   Is Original Cataloging routinely done by Paraprofessional Support Staff? Broken Out by Type of College 54
Table 1.4:   Is Original Cataloging routinely done by Paraprofessional Support Staff? Broken Out by Public or Private Status 54
Table 1.5:   Is Original Cataloging routinely done by Professional Librarians? 54
Table 1.6:   Is Original Cataloging routinely done by Professional Librarians? Broken Out by FTE Student Enrollment 54
Table 1.7:   Is Original Cataloging routinely done by Professional Librarians? Broken Out by Type of College 55
Table 1.8:   Is Original Cataloging routinely done by Professional Librarians? Broken Out by Public or Private Status 55
Table 1.9:   Is Copy Cataloging routinely done by Paraprofessional Support Staff? 55
Table 1.10:   Is Copy Cataloging routinely done by Paraprofessional Support Staff? Broken out by FTE Student Enrollment 55
Table 1.11:   Is Copy Cataloging routinely done by Paraprofessional Support Staff? Broken out by Type of College 55
Table 1.12:   Is Copy Cataloging routinely done by Paraprofessional Support Staff? Broken Out by Public or Private Status 56
Table 1.13:   Is Copy Cataloging routinely done by Professional Librarians?..........................56
Table 1.14:   Is Copy Cataloging routinely done by Professional Librarians? Broken Out by FTE Student Enrollment 56
Table 1.15:   Is Copy Cataloging routinely done by Professional Librarians? Broken Out by Type of College 56
Table 1.16:   Is Copy Cataloging routinely done by Professional Librarians? Broken Out by Public or Private Status..56
Table 1.17:   Is Name Authority Cooperative work (NACO) routinely done by Paraprofessional Support Staff? 56
Table 1.18:   Is Name Authority Cooperative work (NACO) routinely done by Paraprofessional Support Staff? Broken Out by FTE Student Enrollment...............57
Table 1.19:   Is Name Authority Cooperative work (NACO) routinely done by Paraprofessional Support Staff? Broken Out by Type of College 57
Table 1.20:   Is Name Authority Cooperative work (NACO) routinely done by Paraprofessional Support Staff? Broken Out by Public or Private Status 57
Table 1.21:   Is Name Authority Cooperative work (NACO) routinely done by Professional Librarians?..57
Table 1.22:   Is Name Authority Cooperative work (NACO) routinely done by Professional Librarians? Broken Out by FTE Student Enrollment 57
Table 1.23:   Is Name Authority Cooperative work (NACO) routinely done by Professional Librarians? Broken Out by Type of College 58

Table 1.24: Is Name Authority Cooperative work (NACO) routinely done by
Professional Librarians? Broken Out by Public or Private Status............................58

Table 1.25: Is Subject Authority Cooperative Work (SACO) routinely done by
Paraprofessional Support Staff?...58

Table 1.26: Is Subject Authority Cooperative Work (SACO) routinely done by
Paraprofessional Support Staff? Broken Out by FTE Student Enrollment..............58

Table 1.27: Is Subject Authority Cooperative Work (SACO) routinely done by
Paraprofessional Support Staff? Broken Out by Type of College 58

Table 1.28: Is Subject Authority Cooperative Work (SACO) routinely done by
Paraprofessional Support Staff? Broken Out by Public or Private Status 59

Table 1.29: Is Subject Authority Cooperative Work (SACO) routinely done by
Professional Librarians?...59

Table 1.30: Is Subject Authority Cooperative Work (SACO) routinely done by
Professional Librarians? Broken Out by FTE Student Enrollment 59

Table 1.31: Is Subject Authority Cooperative Work (SACO) routinely done by
Professional Librarians? Broken Out by Type of College 59

Table 1.32: Is Subject Authority Cooperative Work (SACO) routinely done by
Professional Librarians? Broken Out by Public or Private Status............................59

Table 1.33: Is Master bibliographic record enhancement in OCLC routinely done by
Paraprofessional Support Staff?...59

Table 1.34: Is Master bibliographic record enhancement in OCLC routinely done by
Paraprofessional Support Staff? Broken Out by FTE Student Enrollment..............60

Table 1.35: Is Master bibliographic record enhancement in OCLC routinely done by
Paraprofessional Support Staff? Broken Out by Type of College 60

Table 1.36: Is Master bibliographic record enhancement in OCLC routinely done by
Paraprofessional Support Staff? Broken Out by Public or Private Status 60

Table 1.37: Is Master bibliographic record enhancement in OCLC routinely done by
Professional Librarians?...60

Table 1.38: Is Master bibliographic record enhancement in OCLC routinely done by
Professional Librarians? Broken Out by FTE Student Enrollment 60

Table 1.39: Is Master bibliographic record enhancement in OCLC routinely done by
Professional Librarians? Broken Out by Type of College.......................................61

Table 1.40: Is Master bibliographic record enhancement in OCLC routinely done by
Professional Librarians? Broken Out by Public or Private Status............................61

Table 1.41: Is participation in PCC, CONSER and BIBCO 1 bibliographic record work
routinely done by Paraprofessional Support Staff? 61

Table 1.42: Is participation in PCC, CONSER and BIBCO 1 bibliographic record work
routinely done by Paraprofessional Support Staff? Broken Out by FTE
Student Enrollment 61

Table 1.43: Is participation in PCC, CONSER and BIBCO 1 bibliographic record work
routinely done by Paraprofessional Support Staff? Broken Out by Type of
College 61

Table 1.44: Is participation in PCC, CONSER and BIBCO 1 bibliographic record work
routinely done by Paraprofessional Support Staff? Broken Out by Public or
Private Status..62

Table 1.45:   Is participation in PCC, CONSER and BIBCO 1 bibliographic record work routinely done by Professional Librarians? 62

Table 1.46:   Is participation in PCC, CONSER and BIBCO 1 bibliographic record work routinely done by Professional Librarians? Broken Out by FTE Student Enrollment..62

Table 1.47:   Is participation in PCC, CONSER and BIBCO 1 bibliographic record work routinely done by Professional Librarians? Broken Out by Type of College...........62

Table 1.48:   Is participation in PCC, CONSER and BIBCO 1 bibliographic record work routinely done by Professional Librarians? Broken Out by Public or Private Status 62

Table 1.49:   Is Master bibliographic record enrichment (adding call numbers, subjects, tables of contents) in OCLC routinely done by Paraprofessional Support Staff? 63

Table 1.50:   Is Master bibliographic record enrichment (adding call numbers, subjects, tables of contents) in OCLC routinely done by Paraprofessional Support Staff? Broken Out by FTE Student Enrollment 63

Table 1.51:   Is Master bibliographic record enrichment (adding call numbers, subjects, tables of contents) in OCLC routinely done by Paraprofessional Support Staff? Broken Out by Type of College 63

Table 1.52:   Is Master bibliographic record enrichment (adding call numbers, subjects, tables of contents) in OCLC routinely done by Paraprofessional Support Staff? Broken Out by Public or Private Status..63

Table 1.53:   Is Master bibliographic record enrichment (adding call numbers, subjects, tables of contents) in OCLC routinely done by Professional Librarians? 63

Table 1.54:   Is Master bibliographic record enrichment (adding call numbers, subjects, tables of contents) in OCLC routinely done by Professional Librarians? Broken Out by FTE Student Enrollment 64

Table 1.55:   Is Master bibliographic record enrichment (adding call numbers, subjects, tables of contents) in OCLC routinely done by Professional Librarians? Broken Out by Type of College 64

Table 1.56:   Is Master bibliographic record enrichment (adding call numbers, subjects, tables of contents) in OCLC routinely done by Professional Librarians? Broken Out by Public or Private Status...64

Table 1.57:   Is Subject analysis and subject heading application routinely done by Paraprofessional Support Staff? 64

Table 1.58:   Is Subject analysis and subject heading application routinely done by Paraprofessional Support Staff? Broken Out by FTE Student Enrollment...............64

Table 1.59:   Is Subject analysis and subject heading application routinely done by Paraprofessional Support Staff? Broken Out by Type of College 65

Table 1.60:   Is Subject analysis and subject heading application routinely done by Paraprofessional Support Staff? Broken Out by Public or Private Status 65

Table 1.61:   Is Subject analysis and subject heading application routinely done by Professional Librarians?...65

Table 1.62:   Is Subject analysis and subject heading application routinely done by Professional Librarians? Broken Out by FTE Student Enrollment 65

Table 1.63:   Is Subject analysis and subject heading application routinely done by
Professional Librarians? Broken Out by Type of College 65
Table 1.64:   Is Subject analysis and subject heading application routinely done by
Professional Librarians? Broken Out by Public or Private Status...........................66
Table 1.65:   Is Classification routinely done by Paraprofessional Support Staff? 66
Table 1.66:   Is Classification routinely done by Paraprofessional Support Staff? Broken
Out by FTE Student Enrollment...66
Table 1.67:   Is Classification routinely done by Paraprofessional Support Staff? Broken
Out by Type of College 66
Table 1.68:   Is Classification routinely done by Paraprofessional Support Staff? Broken
Out by Public or Private Status 66
Table 1.69:   Is Classification routinely done by Professional Librarians?...............................66
Table 1.70:   Is Classification routinely done by Professional Librarians? Broken Out by
FTE Student Enrollment 67
Table 1.71:   Is Classification routinely done by Professional Librarians? Broken Out by
Type of College 67
Table 1.72:   Is Classification routinely done by Professional Librarians? Broken Out by
Public or Private Status..67
Table 1.73:   Are Master bibliographic record upgrades in OCLC routinely done by
Paraprofessional Support Staff? 67
Table 1.74:   Are Master bibliographic record upgrades in OCLC routinely done by
Paraprofessional Support Staff? Broken Out by FTE Student Enrollment..............67
Table 1.75:   Are Master bibliographic record upgrades in OCLC routinely done by
Paraprofessional Support Staff? Broken Out by Type of College 68
Table 1.76:   Are Master bibliographic record upgrades in OCLC routinely done by
Paraprofessional Support Staff? Broken Out by Public or Private Status 68
Table 1.77:   Are Master bibliographic record upgrades in OCLC routinely done by
Professional Librarians?...68
Table 1.78:   Are Master bibliographic record upgrades in OCLC routinely done by
Professional Librarians? Broken Out by FTE Student Enrollment 68
Table 1.79:   Are Master bibliographic record upgrades in OCLC routinely done by
Professional Librarians? Broken Out by Type of College.......................................68
Table 1.80:   Are Master bibliographic record upgrades in OCLC routinely done by
Professional Librarians? Broken Out by Public or Private Status...........................69
Table 1.81:   Is Establishment of local series, uniform title headings and authority records
routinely done by Paraprofessional Support Staff? 69
Table 1.82:   Is Establishment of local series, uniform title headings and authority records
routinely done by Paraprofessional Support Staff? Broken Out by FTE
Student Enrollment 69
Table 1.83:   Is Establishment of local series, uniform title headings and authority records
routinely done by Paraprofessional Support Staff? Broken Out by Type of
College 69
Table 1.84:   Is Establishment of local series, uniform title headings and authority records
routinely done by Paraprofessional Support Staff? Broken Out by Public or
Private Status...69

Table 1.85:   Is Establishment of local series, uniform title headings and authority records routinely done by Professional Librarians? 70

Table 1.86:   Is Establishment of local series, uniform title headings and authority records routinely done by Professional Librarians? Broken Out by FTE Student Enrollment 70

Table 1.87:   Is Establishment of local series, uniform title headings and authority records routinely done by Professional Librarians? Broken Out by Type of College 70

Table 1.88:   Is Establishment of local series, uniform title headings and authority records routinely done by Professional Librarians? Broken Out by Public or Private Status 70

Table 1.89:   Is Establishment of local name, corporate body, and conference headings and authority records routinely done by Paraprofessional Support Staff? 70

Table 1.90:   Is Establishment of local name, corporate body, and conference headings and authority records routinely done by Paraprofessional Support Staff? Broken Out by FTE Student Enrollment 71

Table 1.91:   Is Establishment of local name, corporate body, and conference headings and authority records routinely done by Paraprofessional Support Staff? Broken Out by Type of College 71

Table 1.92:   Is Establishment of local name, corporate body, and conference headings and authority records routinely done by Paraprofessional Support Staff? Broken Out by Public or Private Status 71

Table 1.93:   Is Establishment of local name, corporate body, and conference headings and authority records routinely done by Professional Librarians? 71

Table 1.94:   Is Establishment of local name, corporate body, and conference headings and authority records routinely done by Professional Librarians? Broken Out by FTE Student Enrollment 71

Table 1.95:   Is Establishment of local name, corporate body, and conference headings and authority records routinely done by Professional Librarians? Broken Out by Type of College 72

Table 1.96:   Is Establishment of local name, corporate body, and conference headings and authority records routinely done by Professional Librarians? Broken Out by Public or Private Status 72

Table 1.97:   Is Establishment of local subject and geographic headings and authority records routinely done by Paraprofessional Support Staff? 72

Table 1.98:   Is Establishment of local subject and geographic headings and authority records routinely done by Paraprofessional Support Staff? Broken Out by FTE Student Enrollment 72

Table 1.99:   Is Establishment of local subject and geographic headings and authority records routinely done by Paraprofessional Support Staff? Broken Out by Type of College 72

Table 1.100: Is Establishment of local subject and geographic headings and authority records routinely done by Paraprofessional Support Staff? Broken Out by Public or Private Status 73

Table 1.101: Is Establishment of local subject and geographic headings and authority records routinely done by Professional Librarians? 73

Table 1.102: Is Establishment of local subject and geographic headings and authority records routinely done by Professional Librarians? Broken Out by FTE Student Enrollment 73

Table 1.103: Is Establishment of local subject and geographic headings and authority records routinely done by Professional Librarians? Broken Out by Type of College 73

Table 1.104: Is Establishment of local subject and geographic headings and authority records routinely done by Professional Librarians? Broken Out by Public or Private Status 73

Table 1.105: How many positions in cataloging library support staff has your agency gained or lost in the past five years? 74

Table 1.106: How many positions in cataloging library support staff has your agency gained or lost in the past five years? Broken Out by FTE Student Enrollment 74

Table 1.107: How many positions in cataloging library support staff has your agency gained or lost in the past five years? Broken Out by Type of College 74

Table 1.108: How many positions in cataloging library support staff has your agency gained or lost in the past five years? Broken Out by Public or Private Status..........74

Table 1.109: How many positions for professional librarians in cataloging functions has your agency gained or lost in the past five years? 74

Table 1.110: How many positions for professional librarians in cataloging functions has your agency gained or lost in the past five years? Broken Out by FTE Student Enrollment 75

Table 1.111: How many positions for professional librarians in cataloging functions has your agency gained or lost in the past five years? Broken Out by Type of College 75

Table 1.112: How many positions for professional librarians in cataloging functions has your agency gained or lost in the past five years? Broken Out by Public or Private Status 75

Table 1.113: Does your cataloging agency participate in library school student mentoring or internships, or recruiting existing staff and student workers into the cataloging profession? 75

Table 1.114: Does your cataloging agency participate in library school student mentoring or internships, or recruiting existing staff and student workers into the cataloging profession? Broken Out by FTE Student Enrollment 76

Table 1.115: Does your cataloging agency participate in library school student mentoring or internships, or recruiting existing staff and student workers into the cataloging profession? Broken Out by Type of College 76

Table 1.116: Does your cataloging agency participate in library school student mentoring or internships, or recruiting existing staff and student workers into the cataloging profession? Broken Out by Public or Private Status 76

Table 1.117: Approximately how many of each of the following do you believe will be retiring from your institution within the next five years: Professional Librarians performing mostly cataloging functions? 76

Table 1.118: Approximately how many of each of the following do you believe will be retiring from your institution within the next five years: Professional

Librarians performing mostly cataloging functions? Broken Out by FTE Student Enrollment 77

Table 1.119: Approximately how many of each of the following do you believe will be retiring from your institution within the next five years: Professional Librarians performing mostly cataloging functions? Broken Out by Type of College 77

Table 1.120: Approximately how many of each of the following do you believe will be retiring from your institution within the next five years: Professional Librarians performing mostly cataloging functions? Broken Out by Public or Private Status 77

Table 1.121: Approximately how many of each of the following do you believe will be retiring from your institution within the next five years: Library Paraprofessional Support Staff performing mostly cataloging functions? 77

Table 1.122: Approximately how many of each of the following do you believe will be retiring from your institution within the next five years: Library Paraprofessional Support Staff performing mostly cataloging functions? Broken Out by FTE Student Enrollment 78

Table 1.123: Approximately how many of each of the following do you believe will be retiring from your institution within the next five years: Library Paraprofessional Support Staff performing mostly cataloging functions? Broken Out by Type of College 78

Table 1.124: Approximately how many of each of the following do you believe will be retiring from your institution within the next five years: Library Paraprofessional Support Staff performing mostly cataloging functions? Broken Out by Public or Private Status 78

Table 2.1:   Do catalogers at your institution have salaries comparable to public service librarians? 79

Table 2.2:   Do catalogers at your institution have salaries comparable to public service librarians?? Broken Out by FTE Student Enrollment 79

Table 2.3:   Do catalogers at your institution have salaries comparable to public service librarians?? Broken Out by Type of College 79

Table 2.4:   Do catalogers at your institution have salaries comparable to public service librarians?? Broken Out by Public or Private Status 79

Table 3.1:   Does your technical services area track turn-around time from Acquisitions receipt to Cataloging to shelf-ready distribution? 82

Table 3.2:   Does your technical services area track turn-around time from Acquisitions receipt to Cataloging to shelf-ready distribution? Broken Out by FTE Student Enrollment 82

Table 3.3:   Does your technical services area track turn-around time from Acquisitions receipt to Cataloging to shelf-ready distribution? Broken Out by Type of College 82

Table 3.4:   Does your technical services area track turn-around time from Acquisitions receipt to Cataloging to shelf-ready distribution? Broken Out by Public or Private Status 82

Table 3.5:   How would you rate the use of the following quality indicators in cataloging work: Cataloger or staff work product quotas?..83

Table 3.6:   How would you rate the use of the following quality indicators in cataloging work: Cataloger or staff work product quotas? Broken Out by FTE Student Enrollment..83

Table 3.7:   How would you rate the use of the following quality indicators in cataloging work: Cataloger or staff work product quotas? Broken Out by Type of College 84

Table 3.8:   How would you rate the use of the following quality indicators in cataloging work: Cataloger or staff work product quotas? Broken Out by Public or Private Status...84

Table 3.9:   How would you rate the use of the following quality indicators in cataloging work: Turn-around time from receipt in Cataloging to ready for shelf?.................84

Table 3.10:   How would you rate the use of the following quality indicators in cataloging work: Turn-around time from receipt in Cataloging to ready for shelf? Broken Out by FTE Student Enrollment 84

Table 3.11:   How would you rate the use of the following quality indicators in cataloging work: Turn-around time from receipt in Cataloging to ready for shelf? Broken Out by Type of College 85

Table 3.12:   How would you rate the use of the following quality indicators in cataloging work: Turn-around time from receipt in Cataloging to ready for shelf? Broken Out by Public or Private Status...85

Table 3.13:   How would you rate the use of the following quality indicators in cataloging work: Error rates per bibliographic record?...85

Table 3.14:   How would you rate the use of the following quality indicators in cataloging work: Error rates per bibliographic record? Broken Out by FTE Student Enrollment..85

Table 3.15:   How would you rate the use of the following quality indicators in cataloging work: Error rates per bibliographic record? Broken Out by Type of College 86

Table 3.16:   How would you rate the use of the following quality indicators in cataloging work: Error rates per bibliographic record? Broken Out by Public or Private Status 86

Table 3.17:   How would you rate the use of the following quality indicators in cataloging work: Completeness of bibliographic record? 86

Table 3.18:   How would you rate the use of the following quality indicators in cataloging work: Completeness of bibliographic record? Broken Out by FTE Student Enrollment..86

Table 3.19:   How would you rate the use of the following quality indicators in cataloging work: Completeness of bibliographic record? Broken Out by Type of College 87

Table 3.20:   How would you rate the use of the following quality indicators in cataloging work: Completeness of bibliographic record? Broken Out by Public or Private Status...87

Table 3.21:   How would you rate the use of the following quality indicators in cataloging work: Error rates per authority record?...87

Table 3.22: How would you rate the use of the following quality indicators in cataloging work: Error rates per authority record? Broken Out by FTE Student Enrollment..87

Table 3.23: How would you rate the use of the following quality indicators in cataloging work: Error rates per authority record? Broken Out by Type of College.............88

Table 3.24: How would you rate the use of the following quality indicators in cataloging work: Error rates per authority record? Broken Out by Public or Private Status 88

Table 3.25: How would you rate the use of the following quality indicators in cataloging work: Error rates per holdings record?...88

Table 3.26: How would you rate the use of the following quality indicators in cataloging work: Error rates per holdings record? Broken Out by FTE Student Enrollment..88

Table 3.27: How would you rate the use of the following quality indicators in cataloging work: Error rates per holdings record? Broken Out by Type of College 89

Table 3.28: How would you rate the use of the following quality indicators in cataloging work: Error rates per holdings record? Broken Out by Public or Private Status 89

Table 3.29: How would you rate the use of the following quality indicators in cataloging work: Error rates per physical processing?...89

Table 3.30: How would you rate the use of the following quality indicators in cataloging work: Error rates per physical processing? Broken Out by FTE Student Enrollment..89

Table 3.31: How would you rate the use of the following quality indicators in cataloging work: Error rates per physical processing? Broken Out by Type of College 90

Table 3.32: How would you rate the use of the following quality indicators in cataloging work: Error rates per physical processing? Broken Out by Public or Private Status 90

Table 3.33: How would you rate the use of the following quality indicators in cataloging work: Patron or staff complaints?...90

Table 3.34: How would you rate the use of the following quality indicators in cataloging work: Patron or staff complaints? Broken Out by FTE Student Enrollment............90

Table 3.35: How would you rate the use of the following quality indicators in cataloging work: Patron or staff complaints? Broken Out by Type of College........................91

Table 3.36: How would you rate the use of the following quality indicators in cataloging work: Patron or staff complaints? Broken Out by Public or Private Status..............91

Table 3.37: How would you rate the use of the following quality indicators in cataloging work: Patron or staff commendation?...91

Table 3.38: How would you rate the use of the following quality indicators in cataloging work: Patron or staff commendation? Broken Out by FTE Student Enrollment..91

Table 3.39: How would you rate the use of the following quality indicators in cataloging work: Patron or staff commendation? Broken Out by Type of College...................92

Table 3.40: How would you rate the use of the following quality indicators in cataloging work: Patron or staff commendation? Broken Out by Public or Private Status........92

Table 3.41: How would you rate the use of the following quality indicators in cataloging work: Support or accomplishment of departmental or library goal?........................92

Table 3.42: How would you rate the use of the following quality indicators in cataloging work: Support or accomplishment of departmental or library goal? Broken Out by FTE Student Enrollment..92

Table 3.43: How would you rate the use of the following quality indicators in cataloging work: Support or accomplishment of departmental or library goal? Broken Out by Type of College 93

Table 3.44: How would you rate the use of the following quality indicators in cataloging work: Support or accomplishment of departmental or library goal? Broken Out by Public or Private Status 93

Table 5.1: What functions or value-added services, if any, does your agency outsource to any degree? Authority control: obtaining new and updated authority records 101

Table 5.2: What functions or value-added services, if any, does your agency outsource to any degree? Authority control: obtaining new and updated authority records? Broken Out by FTE Student Enrollment 101

Table 5.3: What functions or value-added services, if any, does your agency outsource to any degree? Authority control: obtaining new and updated authority records? Broken Out by Type of College 101

Table 5.4: What functions or value-added services, if any, does your agency outsource to any degree? Authority control: obtaining new and updated authority records? Broken Out by Public or Private Status...101

Table 5.5: What functions or value-added services, if any, does your agency outsource to any degree? Authority control: updating headings in bibliographic records......101

Table 5.6: What functions or value-added services, if any, does your agency outsource to any degree? Authority control: updating headings in bibliographic records? Broken Out by FTE Student Enrollment 102

Table 5.7: What functions or value-added services, if any, does your agency outsource to any degree? Authority control: updating headings in bibliographic records? Broken Out by Type of College 102

Table 5.8: What functions or value-added services, if any, does your agency outsource to any degree? Authority control: updating headings in bibliographic records? Broken Out by Public or Private Status...102

Table 5.9: What functions or value-added services, if any, does your agency outsource to any degree? Bibliographic records: obtaining new bibliographic records..........102

Table 5.10: What functions or value-added services, if any, does your agency outsource to any degree? obtaining new bibliographic records? Broken Out by FTE Student Enrollment..102

Table 5.11: What functions or value-added services, if any, does your agency outsource to any degree? obtaining new bibliographic records? Broken Out by Type of College 103

Table 5.12: What functions or value-added services, if any, does your agency outsource to any degree? obtaining new bibliographic records? Broken Out by Public or Private Status...103

Table 5.13:   What functions or value-added services, if any, does your agency outsource to any degree? Item records and inventory 103

Table 5.14:   What functions or value-added services, if any, does your agency outsource to any degree? Item records and inventory? Broken Out by FTE Student Enrollment 103

Table 5.15:   What functions or value-added services, if any, does your agency outsource to any degree? Item records and inventory? Broken Out by Type of College 103

Table 5.16:   What functions or value-added services, if any, does your agency outsource to any degree? Item records and inventory? Broken Out by Public or Private Status   104

Table 5.17:   What functions or value-added services, if any, does your agency outsource to any degree? Physical processing and bar-coding 104

Table 5.18:   What functions or value-added services, if any, does your agency outsource to any degree? Physical processing and bar-coding? Broken Out by FTE Student Enrollment 104

Table 5.19:   What functions or value-added services, if any, does your agency outsource to any degree? Physical processing and bar-coding? Broken Out by Type of College   104

Table 5.20:   What functions or value-added services, if any, does your agency outsource to any degree? Physical processing and bar-coding? Broken Out by Public or Private Status 104

Table 5.21:   What functions or value-added services, if any, does your agency outsource to any degree? Table of contents notes added 105

Table 5.22:   What functions or value-added services, if any, does your agency outsource to any degree? Table of contents notes added? Broken Out by FTE Student Enrollment 105

Table 5.23:   What functions or value-added services, if any, does your agency outsource to any degree? Table of contents notes added? Broken Out by Type of College   105

Table 5.24:   What functions or value-added services, if any, does your agency outsource to any degree? Table of contents notes added? Broken Out by Public or Private Status 105

Table 5.25:   What functions or value-added services, if any, does your agency outsource to any degree? Book reviews added 105

Table 5.26:   What functions or value-added services, if any, does your agency outsource to any degree? Book reviews added? Broken Out by FTE Student Enrollment 106

Table 5.27:   What functions or value-added services, if any, does your agency outsource to any degree? Book reviews added? Broken Out by Type of College 106

Table 5.28:   What functions or value-added services, if any, does your agency outsource to any degree? Book reviews added? Broken Out by Public or Private Status 106

Table 5.29:   What functions or value-added services, if any, does your agency outsource to any degree? Book jackets added 106

Table 5.30:   What functions or value-added services, if any, does your agency outsource to any degree? Book jackets added? Broken Out by FTE Student Enrollment 106

Table 5.31:   What functions or value-added services, if any, does your agency outsource to any degree? Book jackets added? Broken Out by Type of College 107

Table 5.32:   What functions or value-added services, if any, does your agency outsource to any degree? Book jackets added? Broken Out by Public or Private Status........ 107

Table 5.33:   What types of library resources are outsourced? Continuing resources (print)...... 107

Table 5.34:   What types of library resources are outsourced? Continuing resources (print)? Broken Out by FTE Student Enrollment 107

Table 5.35:   What types of library resources are outsourced? Continuing resources (print)? Broken Out by Type of College 107

Table 5.36:   What types of library resources are outsourced? Continuing resources (print)? Broken Out by Public or Private Status.. 108

Table 5.37:   What types of library resources are outsourced? E-journals................................ 108

Table 5.38:   What types of library resources are outsourced? E-journals? Broken Out by FTE Student Enrollment 108

Table 5.39:   What types of library resources are outsourced? E-journals? Broken Out by Type of College 108

Table 5.40:   What types of library resources are outsourced? E-journals? Broken Out by Public or Private Status 108

Table 5.41:   What types of library resources are outsourced? E-books................................... 108

Table 5.42:   What types of library resources are outsourced? E-books? Broken Out by FTE Student Enrollment 109

Table 5.43:   What types of library resources are outsourced? E-books? Broken Out by Type of College 109

Table 5.44:   What types of library resources are outsourced? E-books? Broken Out by Public or Private Status.. 109

Table 5.45:   What types of library resources are outsourced? AV Formats 109

Table 5.46:   What types of library resources are outsourced? AV Formats? Broken Out by FTE Student Enrollment 109

Table 5.47:   What types of library resources are outsourced? AV Formats? Broken Out by Type of College 110

Table 5.48:   What types of library resources are outsourced? AV Formats? Broken Out by Public or Private Status.. 110

Table 5.49:   What types of library resources are outsourced? Foreign language resources for which the cataloging agency has no expertise 110

Table 5.50:   What types of library resources are outsourced? Foreign language resources for which the cataloging agency has no expertise? Broken Out by FTE Student Enrollment 110

Table 5.51:   What types of library resources are outsourced? Foreign language resources for which the cataloging agency has no expertise? Broken Out by Type of College   110

Table 5.52:   What types of library resources are outsourced? Foreign language resources for which the cataloging agency has no expertise? Broken Out by Public or Private Status.. 111

Table 5.53:   What types of library resources are outsourced? Other Digital Formats............... 111

Table 5.54:   What types of library resources are outsourced? Other Digital Formats? Broken Out by FTE Student Enrollment 111

Table 5.55:   What types of library resources are outsourced? Other Digital Formats? Broken Out by Type of College 111

Table 5.56:	What types of library resources are outsourced? Other Digital Formats? Broken Out by Public or Private Status 111

Table 5.57:	What types of library resources are outsourced? Materials in Cataloging Backlogs 111

Table 5.58:	What types of library resources are outsourced? Materials in Cataloging Backlogs? Broken Out by FTE Student Enrollment 112

Table 5.59:	What types of library resources are outsourced? Materials in Cataloging Backlogs? Broken Out by Type of College 112

Table 5.60:	What types of library resources are outsourced? Materials in Cataloging Backlogs? Broken Out by Public or Private Status... 112

Table 5.61:	What types of library resources are outsourced? All Materials are outsourced...... 112

Table 5.62:	What quality control methods do you use, if any, to assure vendor supplied records are accurate and complete: Use MarcEdit or other MARC editor to preview records and globally edit to local standards prior to loading? 116

Table 5.63:	What quality control methods do you use, if any, to assure vendor supplied records are accurate and complete: Use MarcEdit or other MARC editor to preview records and globally edit to local standards prior to loading? Broken Out by FTE Student Enrollment.. 116

Table 5.64:	What quality control methods do you use, if any, to assure vendor supplied records are accurate and complete: Use MarcEdit or other MARC editor to preview records and globally edit to local standards prior to loading? Broken Out by Type of College 116

Table 5.65:	What quality control methods do you use, if any, to assure vendor supplied records are accurate and complete: Use MarcEdit or other MARC editor to preview records and globally edit to local standards prior to loading? Broken Out by Public or Private Status 116

Table 5.66:	What quality control methods do you use, if any, to assure vendor supplied records are accurate and complete: Use local integrated system to review loaded records and globally edit to local standards, whenever possible?............... 117

Table 5.67:	What quality control methods do you use, if any, to assure vendor supplied records are accurate and complete: Use local integrated system to review loaded records and globally edit to local standards, whenever possible? Broken Out by FTE Student Enrollment 117

Table 5.68:	What quality control methods do you use, if any, to assure vendor supplied records are accurate and complete: Use local integrated system to review loaded records and globally edit to local standards, whenever possible? Broken Out by Type of College 117

Table 5.69:	What quality control methods do you use, if any, to assure vendor supplied records are accurate and complete: Use local integrated system to review loaded records and globally edit to local standards, whenever possible? Broken Out by Public or Private Status 117

Table 5.70:	What quality control methods do you use, if any, to assure vendor supplied records are accurate and complete: Spot check vendor records, whenever complete review isn't possible? 117

Table 5.71:   What quality control methods do you use, if any, to assure vendor supplied records are accurate and complete: Spot check vendor records, whenever complete review isn't possible? Broken Out by FTE Student Enrollment 118

Table 5.72:   What quality control methods do you use, if any, to assure vendor supplied records are accurate and complete: Spot check vendor records, whenever complete review isn't possible? Broken Out by Type of College 118

Table 5.73:   What quality control methods do you use, if any, to assure vendor supplied records are accurate and complete: Spot check vendor records, whenever complete review isn't possible? Broken Out by Public or Private Status 118

Table 5.74:   What quality control methods do you use, if any, to assure vendor supplied records are accurate and complete: Always spot check all vendor records? 118

Table 5.75:   What quality control methods do you use, if any, to assure vendor supplied records are accurate and complete: Always spot check all vendor records? Broken Out by FTE Student Enrollment 118

Table 5.76:   What quality control methods do you use, if any, to assure vendor supplied records are accurate and complete: Always spot check all vendor records? Broken Out by Type of College 119

Table 5.77:   What quality control methods do you use, if any, to assure vendor supplied records are accurate and complete: Always spot check all vendor records? Broken Out by Public or Private Status 119

Table 5.78:   What quality control methods do you use, if any, to assure vendor supplied records are accurate and complete: No or minimal review performed? 119

Table 5.79:   What quality control methods do you use, if any, to assure vendor supplied records are accurate and complete: No or minimal review performed? Broken Out by FTE Student Enrollment 119

Table 5.80:   What quality control methods do you use, if any, to assure vendor supplied records are accurate and complete: No or minimal review performed? Broken Out by Type of College 120

Table 5.81:   What quality control methods do you use, if any, to assure vendor supplied records are accurate and complete: No or minimal review performed? Broken Out by Public or Private Status 120

Table 6.1:   Please categorize the preparedness of your recent library hires in the following cataloging and metadata competencies, philosophies, principles and practices: Classification Systems? 124

Table 6.2:   Please categorize the preparedness of your recent library hires in the following cataloging and metadata competencies, philosophies, principles and practices: Classification Systems? Broken Out by FTE Student Enrollment 124

Table 6.3:   Please categorize the preparedness of your recent library hires in the following cataloging and metadata competencies, philosophies, principles and practices: Classification Systems? Broken Out by Type of College 124

Table 6.4:   Please categorize the preparedness of your recent library hires in the following cataloging and metadata competencies, philosophies, principles and practices: Classification Systems? Broken Out by Public or Private Status 125

Table 6.5:   Please categorize the preparedness of your recent library hires in the following cataloging and metadata competencies, philosophies, principles and practices: Subject /Genre Thesauri Systems?.. 125

Table 6.6:   Please categorize the preparedness of your recent library hires in the following cataloging and metadata competencies, philosophies, principles and practices: Subject /Genre Thesauri Systems? Broken Out by FTE Student Enrollment 125

Table 6.7:   Please categorize the preparedness of your recent library hires in the following cataloging and metadata competencies, philosophies, principles and practices: Subject /Genre Thesauri Systems? Broken Out by Type of College 125

Table 6.8:   Please categorize the preparedness of your recent library hires in the following cataloging and metadata competencies, philosophies, principles and practices: Subject /Genre Thesauri Systems? Broken Out by Public or Private Status.. 126

Table 6.9:   Please categorize the preparedness of your recent library hires in the following cataloging and metadata competencies, philosophies, principles and practices: Classification and Subject /Genre Analysis Principles, Rules and Tools?... 126

Table 6.10:   Please categorize the preparedness of your recent library hires in the following cataloging and metadata competencies, philosophies, principles and practices: Classification and Subject /Genre Analysis Principles, Rules and Tools? Broken Out by FTE Student Enrollment 126

Table 6.11:   Please categorize the preparedness of your recent library hires in the following cataloging and metadata competencies, philosophies, principles and practices: Classification and Subject /Genre Analysis Principles, Rules and Tools? Broken Out by Type of College 126

Table 6.12:   Please categorize the preparedness of your recent library hires in the following cataloging and metadata competencies, philosophies, principles and practices: Classification and Subject /Genre Analysis Principles, Rules and Tools? Broken Out by Public or Private Status... 127

Table 6.13:   Please categorize the preparedness of your recent library hires in the following cataloging and metadata competencies, philosophies, principles and practices: Java and PERL Script Applications?... 127

Table 6.14:   Please categorize the preparedness of your recent library hires in the following cataloging and metadata competencies, philosophies, principles and practices: Java and PERL Script Applications? Broken Out by FTE Student Enrollment 127

Table 6.15:   Please categorize the preparedness of your recent library hires in the following cataloging and metadata competencies, philosophies, principles and practices: Java and PERL Script Applications? Broken Out by Type of College 127

Table 6.16:   Please categorize the preparedness of your recent library hires in the following cataloging and metadata competencies, philosophies, principles and practices: Java and PERL Script Applications? Broken Out by Public or Private Status.. 128

Table 6.17:   Please categorize the preparedness of your recent library hires in the following cataloging and metadata competencies, philosophies, principles and practices: Cataloging Rules and Tools (including Descriptive Cataloging......128

Table 6.18:   Please categorize the preparedness of your recent library hires in the following cataloging and metadata competencies, philosophies, principles and practices: Cataloging Rules and Tools (including Descriptive Cataloging)? Broken Out by FTE Student Enrollment..........................128

Table 6.19:   Please categorize the preparedness of your recent library hires in the following cataloging and metadata competencies, philosophies, principles and practices: Cataloging Rules and Tools (including Descriptive Cataloging)? Broken Out by Type of College 128

Table 6.20:   Please categorize the preparedness of your recent library hires in the following cataloging and metadata competencies, philosophies, principles and practices: Cataloging Rules and Tools (including Descriptive Cataloging)? Broken Out by Public or Private Status 129

Table 6.21:   Please categorize the preparedness of your recent library hires in the following cataloging and metadata competencies, philosophies, principles and practices: Information Technology and Social Behavior in the Organizational Context? 129

Table 6.22:   Please categorize the preparedness of your recent library hires in the following cataloging and metadata competencies, philosophies, principles and practices: Information Technology and Social Behavior in the Organizational Context? Broken Out by FTE Student Enrollment........................129

Table 6.23:   Please categorize the preparedness of your recent library hires in the following cataloging and metadata competencies, philosophies, principles and practices: Information Technology and Social Behavior in the Organizational Context? Broken Out by Type of College....................129

Table 6.24:   Please categorize the preparedness of your recent library hires in the following cataloging and metadata competencies, philosophies, principles and practices: Information Technology and Social Behavior in the Organizational Context? Broken Out by Public or Private Status 130

Table 6.25:   Please categorize the preparedness of your recent library hires in the following cataloging and metadata competencies, philosophies, principles and practices: Metadata standards for Digital Resources (Dublin Core, MODS, VRA, Open Archives Initiative, etc.)?..................................130

Table 6.26:   Please categorize the preparedness of your recent library hires in the following cataloging and metadata competencies, philosophies, principles and practices: Metadata standards for Digital Resources (Dublin Core, MODS, VRA, Open Archives Initiative, etc.)? Broken Out by FTE Student Enrollment..130

Table 6.27:   Please categorize the preparedness of your recent library hires in the following cataloging and metadata competencies, philosophies, principles and practices: Metadata standards for Digital Resources (Dublin Core, MODS, VRA, Open Archives Initiative, etc.)? Broken Out by Type of College 131

Table 6.28: Please categorize the preparedness of your recent library hires in the following cataloging and metadata competencies, philosophies, principles and practices: Metadata standards for Digital Resources (Dublin Core, MODS, VRA, Open Archives Initiative, etc.) Broken Out by Public or Private Status..131

Table 6.29: Please categorize the preparedness of your recent library hires in the following cataloging and metadata competencies, philosophies, principles and practices: Abstracting and Indexing?...131

Table 6.30: Please categorize the preparedness of your recent library hires in the following cataloging and metadata competencies, philosophies, principles and practices: Abstracting and Indexing? Broken Out by FTE Student Enrollment...131

Table 6.31: Please categorize the preparedness of your recent library hires in the following cataloging and metadata competencies, philosophies, principles and practices: Abstracting and Indexing? Broken Out by Type of College...........132

Table 6.32: Please categorize the preparedness of your recent library hires in the following cataloging and metadata competencies, philosophies, principles and practices: Abstracting and Indexing? Broken Out by Public or Private Status 132

Table 6.33: Please categorize the preparedness of your recent library hires in the following cataloging and metadata competencies, philosophies, principles and practices: Electronic delivery of Services?...132

Table 6.34: Please categorize the preparedness of your recent library hires in the following cataloging and metadata competencies, philosophies, principles and practices: Electronic delivery of Services? Broken Out by FTE Student Enrollment...132

Table 6.35: Please categorize the preparedness of your recent library hires in the following cataloging and metadata competencies, philosophies, principles and practices: Electronic delivery of Services? Broken Out by Type of College 133

Table 6.36: Please categorize the preparedness of your recent library hires in the following cataloging and metadata competencies, philosophies, principles and practices: Electronic delivery of Services? Broken Out by Public or Private Status..133

Table 6.37: Please categorize the preparedness of your recent library hires in the following cataloging and metadata competencies, philosophies, principles and practices: Technical Services in Libraries? 133

Table 6.38: Please categorize the preparedness of your recent library hires in the following cataloging and metadata competencies, philosophies, principles and practices: Technical Services in Libraries? Broken Out by FTE Student Enrollment...133

Table 6.39: Please categorize the preparedness of your recent library hires in the following cataloging and metadata competencies, philosophies, principles and practices: Technical Services in Libraries? Broken Out by Type of College 134

Table 6.40: Please categorize the preparedness of your recent library hires in the following cataloging and metadata competencies, philosophies, principles and practices: Technical Services in Libraries? Broken Out by Public or Private Status... 134

Table 6.41: Please categorize the preparedness of your recent library hires in the following cataloging and metadata competencies, philosophies, principles and practices: Web and Local Network System Administration and Management? 134

Table 6.42: Please categorize the preparedness of your recent library hires in the following cataloging and metadata competencies, philosophies, principles and practices: Web and Local Network System Administration and Management? Broken Out by FTE Student Enrollment......................... 135

Table 6.43: Please categorize the preparedness of your recent library hires in the following cataloging and metadata competencies, philosophies, principles and practices: Web and Local Network System Administration and Management? Broken Out by Type of College 135

Table 6.44: Please categorize the preparedness of your recent library hires in the following cataloging and metadata competencies, philosophies, principles and practices: Web and Local Network System Administration and Management? Broken Out by Public or Private Status 135

Table 6.45: Please categorize the preparedness of your recent library hires in the following cataloging and metadata competencies, philosophies, principles and practices: Cataloging Formats - Books?...................................... 135

Table 6.46: Please categorize the preparedness of your recent library hires in the following cataloging and metadata competencies, philosophies, principles and practices: Cataloging Formats - Books? Broken Out by FTE Student Enrollment... 136

Table 6.47: Please categorize the preparedness of your recent library hires in the following cataloging and metadata competencies, philosophies, principles and practices: Cataloging Formats - Books? Broken Out by Type of College 136

Table 6.48: Please categorize the preparedness of your recent library hires in the following cataloging and metadata competencies, philosophies, principles and practices: Cataloging Formats - Books? Broken Out by Public or Private Status 136

Table 6.49: Please categorize the preparedness of your recent library hires in the following cataloging and metadata competencies, philosophies, principles and practices: Cataloging Formats - Non Books, Digital Resources?.................... 136

Table 6.50: Please categorize the preparedness of your recent library hires in the following cataloging and metadata competencies, philosophies, principles and practices: Cataloging Formats - Non Books, Digital Resources? Broken Out by FTE Student Enrollment.. 137

Table 6.51: Please categorize the preparedness of your recent library hires in the following cataloging and metadata competencies, philosophies, principles and practices: Cataloging Formats - Non Books, Digital Resources? Broken Out by Type of College 137

Table 6.52: Please categorize the preparedness of your recent library hires in the following cataloging and metadata competencies, philosophies, principles and practices: Cataloging Formats - Non Books, Digital Resources? Broken Out by Public or Private Status 137

Table 6.53: Please categorize the preparedness of your recent library hires in the following cataloging and metadata competencies, philosophies, principles and practices: Cataloging Formats - Continuing and Integrating Resources? 137

Table 6.54: Please categorize the preparedness of your recent library hires in the following cataloging and metadata competencies, philosophies, principles and practices: Cataloging Formats - Continuing and Integrating Resources? Broken Out by FTE Student Enrollment 138

Table 6.55: Please categorize the preparedness of your recent library hires in the following cataloging and metadata competencies, philosophies, principles and practices: Cataloging Formats - Continuing and Integrating Resources? Broken Out by Type of College 138

Table 6.56: Please categorize the preparedness of your recent library hires in the following cataloging and metadata competencies, philosophies, principles and practices: Cataloging Formats - Continuing and Integrating Resources? Broken Out by Public or Private Status...138

Table 6.57: Please categorize the preparedness of your recent library hires in the following cataloging and metadata competencies, philosophies, principles and practices: Cataloging Special Materials – Law?..138

Table 6.58: Please categorize the preparedness of your recent library hires in the following cataloging and metadata competencies, philosophies, principles and practices: Cataloging Special Materials - Law? Broken Out by FTE Student Enrollment 139

Table 6.59: Please categorize the preparedness of your recent library hires in the following cataloging and metadata competencies, philosophies, principles and practices: Cataloging Special Materials - Law? Broken Out by Type of College 139

Table 6.60: Please categorize the preparedness of your recent library hires in the following cataloging and metadata competencies, philosophies, principles and practices: Cataloging Special Materials - Law? Broken Out by Public or Private Status..139

Table 6.61: Please categorize the preparedness of your recent library hires in the following cataloging and metadata competencies, philosophies, principles and practices: Cataloging Special Materials – Music?..139

Table 6.62: Please categorize the preparedness of your recent library hires in the following cataloging and metadata competencies, philosophies, principles and practices: Cataloging Special Materials - Music? Broken Out by FTE Student Enrollment 140

Table 6.63: Please categorize the preparedness of your recent library hires in the following cataloging and metadata competencies, philosophies, principles and practices: Cataloging Special Materials - Music? Broken Out by Type of College 140

Table 6.64: Please categorize the preparedness of your recent library hires in the following cataloging and metadata competencies, philosophies, principles and practices: Cataloging Special Materials - Music? Broken Out by Public or Private Status..140

Table 6.65: Please categorize the preparedness of your recent library hires in the following cataloging and metadata competencies, philosophies, principles and practices: Cataloging Special Materials - Archives and Rare Materials?........140

Table 6.66: Please categorize the preparedness of your recent library hires in the following cataloging and metadata competencies, philosophies, principles and practices: Cataloging Special Materials - Archives and Rare Materials? Broken Out by FTE Student Enrollment 141

Table 6.67: Please categorize the preparedness of your recent library hires in the following cataloging and metadata competencies, philosophies, principles and practices: Cataloging Special Materials - Archives and Rare Materials? Broken Out by Type of College 141

Table 6.68: Please categorize the preparedness of your recent library hires in the following cataloging and metadata competencies, philosophies, principles and practices: Cataloging Special Materials - Archives and Rare Materials? Broken Out by Public or Private Status..141

Table 6.69: Please categorize the preparedness of your recent library hires in the following cataloging and metadata competencies, philosophies, principles and practices: XML and/or XSLT? 141

Table 6.70: Please categorize the preparedness of your recent library hires in the following cataloging and metadata competencies, philosophies, principles and practices: XML and/or XSLT? Broken Out by FTE Student Enrollment........142

Table 6.71: Please categorize the preparedness of your recent library hires in the following cataloging and metadata competencies, philosophies, principles and practices: XML and/or XSLT? Broken Out by Type of College 142

Table 6.72: Please categorize the preparedness of your recent library hires in the following cataloging and metadata competencies, philosophies, principles and practices: XML and/or XSLT? Broken Out by Public or Private Status.........142

Table 6.73: Please categorize the preparedness of your recent library hires in the following cataloging and metadata competencies, philosophies, principles and practices: Economics and Metrics of Information? 142

Table 6.74: Please categorize the preparedness of your recent library hires in the following cataloging and metadata competencies, philosophies, principles and practices: Economics and Metrics of Information? Broken Out by FTE Student Enrollment 143

Table 6.75: Please categorize the preparedness of your recent library hires in the following cataloging and metadata competencies, philosophies, principles and practices: Economics and Metrics of Information? Broken Out by Type of College 143

Table 6.76: Please categorize the preparedness of your recent library hires in the following cataloging and metadata competencies, philosophies, principles and practices: Economics and Metrics of Information? Broken Out by Public or Private Status..143

Table 6.77:   Please categorize the preparedness of your recent library hires in the following cataloging and metadata competencies, philosophies, principles and practices: Discovery Tools and Applications? 143

Table 6.78:   Please categorize the preparedness of your recent library hires in the following cataloging and metadata competencies, philosophies, principles and practices: Discovery Tools and Applications? Broken Out by FTE Student Enrollment 144

Table 6.79:   Please categorize the preparedness of your recent library hires in the following cataloging and metadata competencies, philosophies, principles and practices: Discovery Tools and Applications? Broken Out by Type of College 144

Table 6.80:   Please categorize the preparedness of your recent library hires in the following cataloging and metadata competencies, philosophies, principles and practices: Discovery Tools and Applications? Broken Out by Public or Private Status..144

Table 6.81:   Please categorize the preparedness of your recent library hires in the following cataloging and metadata competencies, philosophies, principles and practices: Authority Control? 144

Table 6.82:   Please categorize the preparedness of your recent library hires in the following cataloging and metadata competencies, philosophies, principles and practices: Authority Control? Broken Out by FTE Student Enrollment..........145

Table 6.83:   Please categorize the preparedness of your recent library hires in the following cataloging and metadata competencies, philosophies, principles and practices: Authority Control? Broken Out by Type of College.....................145

Table 6.84:   Please categorize the preparedness of your recent library hires in the following cataloging and metadata competencies, philosophies, principles and practices: Authority Control? Broken Out by Public or Private Status 145

Table 6.85:   Please categorize the preparedness of your recent library hires in the following cataloging and metadata competencies, philosophies, principles and practices: Web Usability, User Research, and Human Interface Design? 145

Table 6.86:   Please categorize the preparedness of your recent library hires in the following cataloging and metadata competencies, philosophies, principles and practices: Web Usability, User Research, and Human Interface Design? Broken Out by FTE Student Enrollment 146

Table 6.87:   Please categorize the preparedness of your recent library hires in the following cataloging and metadata competencies, philosophies, principles and practices: Web Usability, User Research, and Human Interface Design? Broken Out by Type of College 146

Table 6.88:   Please categorize the preparedness of your recent library hires in the following cataloging and metadata competencies, philosophies, principles and practices: Web Usability, User Research, and Human Interface Design? Broken Out by Public or Private Status..146

Table 6.89:   Please categorize the preparedness of your recent library hires in the following cataloging and metadata competencies, philosophies, principles and practices: International MARC Bibliographic, Authority and Holdings Standards? 146

Table 6.90: Please categorize the preparedness of your recent library hires in the following cataloging and metadata competencies, philosophies, principles and practices: International MARC Bibliographic, Authority and Holdings Standards? Broken Out by FTE Student Enrollment..147

Table 6.91: Please categorize the preparedness of your recent library hires in the following cataloging and metadata competencies, philosophies, principles and practices: International MARC Bibliographic, Authority and Holdings Standards? Broken Out by Type of College 147

Table 6.92: Please categorize the preparedness of your recent library hires in the following cataloging and metadata competencies, philosophies, principles and practices: International MARC Bibliographic, Authority and Holdings Standards? Broken Out by Public or Private Status 147

Table 6.93: Please categorize the preparedness of your recent library hires in the following cataloging and metadata competencies, philosophies, principles and practices: Data Modeling, Warehousing, Mining? 147

Table 6.94: Please categorize the preparedness of your recent library hires in the following cataloging and metadata competencies, philosophies, principles and practices: Data Modeling, Warehousing, Mining? Broken Out by FTE Student Enrollment 148

Table 6.95: Please categorize the preparedness of your recent library hires in the following cataloging and metadata competencies, philosophies, principles and practices: Data Modeling, Warehousing, Mining? Broken Out by Type of College 148

Table 6.96: Please categorize the preparedness of your recent library hires in the following cataloging and metadata competencies, philosophies, principles and practices: Data Modeling, Warehousing, Mining? Broken Out by Public or Private Status...148

Table 6.97: Please categorize the preparedness of your recent library hires in the following cataloging and metadata competencies, philosophies, principles and practices: Information Systems Analysis?....................................148

Table 6.98: Please categorize the preparedness of your recent library hires in the following cataloging and metadata competencies, philosophies, principles and practices: Information Systems Analysis? Broken Out by FTE Student Enrollment..149

Table 6.99: Please categorize the preparedness of your recent library hires in the following cataloging and metadata competencies, philosophies, principles and practices: Information Systems Analysis? Broken Out by Type of College 149

Table 6.100: Please categorize the preparedness of your recent library hires in the following cataloging and metadata competencies, philosophies, principles and practices: Information Systems Analysis? Broken Out by Public or Private Status...149

Table 6.101: Please categorize the preparedness of your recent library hires in the following cataloging and metadata competencies, philosophies, principles and practices: Programming Languages and Applications? 149

Table 6.102: Please categorize the preparedness of your recent library hires in the following cataloging and metadata competencies, philosophies, principles and practices: Programming Languages and Applications? Broken Out by FTE Student Enrollment 150

Table 6.103: Please categorize the preparedness of your recent library hires in the following cataloging and metadata competencies, philosophies, principles and practices: Programming Languages and Applications? Broken Out by Type of College 150

Table 6.104: Please categorize the preparedness of your recent library hires in the following cataloging and metadata competencies, philosophies, principles and practices: Programming Languages and Applications? Broken Out by Public or Private Status...150

Table 6.105: Please categorize the preparedness of your recent library hires in the following cataloging and metadata competencies, philosophies, principles and practices: Relational Database Design? 150

Table 6.106: Please categorize the preparedness of your recent library hires in the following cataloging and metadata competencies, philosophies, principles and practices: Relational Database Design? Broken Out by FTE Student Enrollment 151

Table 6.107: Please categorize the preparedness of your recent library hires in the following cataloging and metadata competencies, philosophies, principles and practices: Relational Database Design? Broken Out by Type of College........151

Table 6.108: Please categorize the preparedness of your recent library hires in the following cataloging and metadata competencies, philosophies, principles and practices: Relational Database Design? Broken Out by Public or Private Status 151

Table 6.109: Please categorize the preparedness of your recent library hires in the following cataloging and metadata competencies, philosophies, principles and practices: OCLC Systems and Services?..151

Table 6.110: Please categorize the preparedness of your recent library hires in the following cataloging and metadata competencies, philosophies, principles and practices: OCLC Systems and Services? Broken Out by FTE Student Enrollment 152

Table 6.111: Please categorize the preparedness of your recent library hires in the following cataloging and metadata competencies, philosophies, principles and practices: OCLC Systems and Services? Broken Out by Type of College......152

Table 6.112: Please categorize the preparedness of your recent library hires in the following cataloging and metadata competencies, philosophies, principles and practices: OCLC Systems and Services? Broken Out by Public or Private Status 152

Table 6.113: Please categorize the preparedness of your recent library hires in the following cataloging and metadata competencies, philosophies, principles and practices: Digital Libraries and Collections?..152

Table 6.114: Please categorize the preparedness of your recent library hires in the following cataloging and metadata competencies, philosophies, principles and practices: Digital Libraries and Collections? Broken Out by FTE Student Enrollment 153

Table 6.115: Please categorize the preparedness of your recent library hires in the following cataloging and metadata competencies, philosophies, principles and practices: Digital Libraries and Collections? Broken Out by Type of College 153

Table 6.116: Please categorize the preparedness of your recent library hires in the following cataloging and metadata competencies, philosophies, principles and practices: Digital Libraries and Collections? Broken Out by Public or Private Status... 153

Table 6.117: Please categorize the preparedness of your recent library hires in the following cataloging and metadata competencies, philosophies, principles and practices: Practicum: Experiential Learning?.. 153

Table 6.118: Please categorize the preparedness of your recent library hires in the following cataloging and metadata competencies, philosophies, principles and practices: Practicum: Experiential Learning? Broken Out by FTE Student Enrollment.. 154

Table 6.119: Please categorize the preparedness of your recent library hires in the following cataloging and metadata competencies, philosophies, principles and practices: Experiential Learning? Broken Out by Type of College................ 154

Table 6.120: Please categorize the preparedness of your recent library hires in the following cataloging and metadata competencies, philosophies, principles and practices: Experiential Learning? Broken Out by Public or Private Status 154

Table 6.121: Please categorize the preparedness of your recent library hires in the following cataloging and metadata competencies, philosophies, principles and practices: Information Storage, Retrieval, Architecture?............................... 154

Table 6.122: Please categorize the preparedness of your recent library hires in the following cataloging and metadata competencies, philosophies, principles and practices: Information Storage, Retrieval, Architecture? Broken Out by FTE Student Enrollment 155

Table 6.123: Please categorize the preparedness of your recent library hires in the following cataloging and metadata competencies, philosophies, principles and practices: Information Storage, Retrieval, Architecture? Broken Out by Type of College 155

Table 6.124: Please categorize the preparedness of your recent library hires in the following cataloging and metadata competencies, philosophies, principles and practices: Information Storage, Retrieval, Architecture? Broken Out by Public or Private Status... 155

Table 6.125: Please categorize the preparedness of your recent library hires in the following cataloging and metadata competencies, philosophies, principles and practices: Social Networking and Information? 155

Table 6.126: Please categorize the preparedness of your recent library hires in the following cataloging and metadata competencies, philosophies, principles and practices: Social Networking and Information? Broken Out by FTE Student Enrollment... 156

Table 6.127: Please categorize the preparedness of your recent library hires in the following cataloging and metadata competencies, philosophies, principles and practices: Social Networking and Information? Broken Out by Type of College 156

Table 6.128: Please categorize the preparedness of your recent library hires in the following cataloging and metadata competencies, philosophies, principles and practices: Social Networking and Information? Broken Out by Public or Private Status.. 156

Table 6.129: Please categorize the preparedness of your recent library hires in the following cataloging and metadata competencies, philosophies, principles and practices: Electronic Publishing and Scholarly Communication?................... 156

Table 6.130: Please categorize the preparedness of your recent library hires in the following cataloging and metadata competencies, philosophies, principles and practices: Electronic Publishing and Scholarly Communication? Broken Out by FTE Student Enrollment.. 157

Table 6.131: Please categorize the preparedness of your recent library hires in the following cataloging and metadata competencies, philosophies, principles and practices: Electronic Publishing and Scholarly Communication? Broken Out by Type of College 157

Table 6.132: Please categorize the preparedness of your recent library hires in the following cataloging and metadata competencies, philosophies, principles and practices: Electronic Publishing and Scholarly Communication? Broken Out by Public or Private Status 157

Table 6.133: Please categorize the preparedness of your recent library hires in the following cataloging and metadata competencies, philosophies, principles and practices: Principles of Historical and Contemporary Bibliographic Control? 157

Table 6.134: Please categorize the preparedness of your recent library hires in the following cataloging and metadata competencies, philosophies, principles and practices: Principles of Historical and Contemporary Bibliographic Control? Broken Out by FTE Student Enrollment.............................. 158

Table 6.135: Please categorize the preparedness of your recent library hires in the following cataloging and metadata competencies, philosophies, principles and practices: Principles of Historical and Contemporary Bibliographic Control? Broken Out by Type of College.. 158

Table 6.136: Please categorize the preparedness of your recent library hires in the following cataloging and metadata competencies, philosophies, principles and practices: Principles of Historical and Contemporary Bibliographic Control? Broken Out by Public or Private Status.............................. 158

SURVEY PARTICIPANTS

Arizona State University
Athens State University Library
Auburn University
Auburn University Libraries
Augusta State University
Barry University School of Law Library
Brock University
Calvin College
CCBC
City University of Seattle, Library Services
Clark University
Clemson University
Colgate University
Colorado Christian University
Eckerd College
Franciscan University of Steubenville
Furman University
Geneva College - McCartney Library
Georgetown College, Ensor Learning Resource Center
Georgetown University Library
Greenfield Community College
Haverford College
John Abbott College
Joint Forces Staff College
Kingston University
LaGrange College
Lane Library -- Ripon College
Lehigh University
Lehigh University Libraries
Lincoln University (PA)
Merced College
Messiah College
Michigan State University
Mohawk Valley Community College
Motlow State Community College
Mount Saint Mary College
Nassau Community College
Nelson Poynter Memorial Library, University of South Florida St. Petersburg
North Carolina State University Libraries
Northern Michigan University Olson Library
Northwest University
Ohio University Libraries
Paris Junior College

Paul Meek Library, University of Tennessee at Martin
Pellissippi State
Penn State Libraries
Radford University-McConnell Library
Regent University
Robert Morris University
Saint Louis University Law Library
Saint Mary's College, Notre Dame, Indiana
Simpson College
Stanly Community College
Syracuse University Library
Texas State University-San Marcos
The University of Findlay
Univ. of NV, Las Vegas Libraries
University of Central Arkansas
University of Denver
University of Mississippi Libraries
University of Missouri-Kansas City
University of New Mexico
University of Northern Iowa
University of Pittsburgh, Health Sciences Library System
University of South Alabama
University of West Georgia
Wayne State College
Wayne State University
Western Washington University
William & Mary

CHARACTERISTICS OF THE SAMPLE

FTE Student Enrollment

	Less than 2,000	2,000 to 5,000	5,000 to 10,000	Over 10,000
Entire Sample	20.00%	25.71%	22.86%	31.43%

Type of College

	Community College	4-Year Degree Granting College	MA or PHD Level Carnegie Class Institution	Level 1 or Level 2 Carnegie Class Research University
Entire Sample	14.29%	41.43%	22.86%	21.43%

Public or Private Status

	Public	Private
Entire Sample	60.00%	40.00%

SUMMARY OF MAIN FINDINGS

1. Personnel Issues

In 31.43% of academic libraries, original cataloging was routinely performed by paraprofessional support staff. In colleges with greater student enrollment, paraprofessionals had a greater hand in original cataloging, with 54.55% of paraprofessionals in colleges with more than 10,000 students routinely performing this task, while only 7.14% of paraprofessionals in colleges with less than 2,000 students did so. While only 10% of community colleges had these staff members performing original cataloging, 60% of level 1 and level 2 Carnegie Class research universities did, and the percentage of paraprofessionals who routinely carried out this work was commensurate with the level of degree granted by the college. 38.10% of paraprofessionals performed this task in public colleges, and 21.43% in private colleges.

Original cataloging was routinely performed by professional librarians in 88.57% of academic libraries, least so in MA and PHD level Carnegie Class institutions, 75% of which had professional librarians regularly performing this task. 92.86% of private colleges had librarians performing original cataloging, approximately 7% more than in public colleges.

Copy cataloging was routinely performed by paraprofessionals in 81.43% of libraries in the sample, and by librarians in 58.57% of them. Paraprofessionals did copy cataloging least in colleges with less than 2,000 students, 64.29% of which had them performing this task. In these same college libraries, 71.43 % of librarians performed this work, compared to 50% of colleges with 5,000 to 10,000 students, and 55.55% of colleges with over 10,000 students. Paraprofessionals routinely did copy cataloging in 50% of community colleges and in 100% of level 1 and 2 Carnegie Class research universities.

Paraprofessionals performed Name Authority Cooperative (NACO) work in 11.43% of college libraries and only in public colleges with more than 5,000 current students. Paraprofessionals did NACO work in 33.33% of level 1 and 2 Carnegie Class research universities, and in 0% of 4-year degree granting colleges. NACO work was routinely performed by professional librarians in 45.71% of libraries in the sample. Librarians in 80% of level 1 and level 2 Carnegie Class research universities did NACO work, whereas 30% of librarians in community colleges did the same.

Subject Authority Cooperative (SACO) work was also performed by 11.43% of paraprofessionals in academic libraries, and again, only in colleges with more than 5,000 students. 16.67% of public colleges had paraprofessionals performing this work regularly, and 3.57% of private colleges. Professional librarians did SACO work in 32.86% of academic libraries, including 35.71% of public colleges and 28.57% of private ones. As much as 38.89% of colleges with 2,000 to 5,000 students had librarians performing this kind of work, and 53.33% of level 1 and 2 Carnegie Class Research Universities.

Master bibliographic record enhancement in OCLC was performed by paraprofessional support staff in 30% of academic libraries, and by professional librarians in 75.71% of academic libraries. Paraprofessionals did the most bibliographic record enhancement in colleges with over 10,000 students, 45.45% of which had them performing this task. Only 7.14% of colleges with less than 2,000 students had paraprofessionals doing this work, and no community colleges did. Meanwhile, professional librarians performed enhancement work in 93.33% of level 1 and level 2 Carnegie Class research universities, and in 89.29% of all private colleges in the sample.

10% of libraries in the sample had paraprofessionals routinely participate in PCC, CONSER, or BIBCO 1 bibliographic record work. 22.86% of academic libraries had professional librarians doing this work, though only 5.56% of libraries with between 2,000 and 5,000 students, and 6.9% of 4-year degree granting colleges. Librarians participated in PCC, CONSER, or BIBCO 1 bibliographic record work in 30.95% of public colleges and 10.71% of private colleges, many in level 1 and 2 Carnegie Class research universities, 46.67% of which had librarians carry out this work.

Master bibliographic record enrichment (adding call numbers, subjects, table of contents) in OCLC was performed by paraprofessionals in 32.86% of libraries, and by 67.14 of professional librarians. As much as 85.71% of colleges with student enrollment less than 2,000 had librarians performing this task and 78.57% of all private colleges in the sample. 59.52% of public colleges had librarians doing this work, and 30.95% of these same colleges had paraprofessionals doing it. 75.86% of all 4-year degree granting colleges had librarians performing enrichment work.

Paraprofessional personnel performed subject analysis and subject heading application in 38.57% of college libraries, including 46.43% of private colleges and 60% of level 1 and 2 Carnegie Class research universities. These percentages fall to 33.33% for public libraries and 10% for community colleges. Professional librarians performed subject analysis and subject heading application in 83.43% of academic libraries. This work was performed by librarians in 92.86% of colleges with less than 2,000 students and decreasingly in larger colleges. Librarians routinely performed this work in 86.21% of 4-year degree granting colleges, and more so in level 1 and level 2 Carnegie Class research universities.

Classification was performed by professional librarians in 88.57% of college libraries, and by paraprofessionals in 44.29%. The disparity was greatest in community colleges, 100% of which had librarians performing this work and only 20% of which had paraprofessionals doing it. Similarly, 100% of colleges with less than 2,000 students had librarians doing classification work, while only 35.71% of them had paraprofessionals completing the same task. Librarians did classification work in 76.19% of public colleges and 89.29% of private colleges.

Librarians also did a greater share of master bibliographic record upgrades in OCLC than paraprofessionals did. 65.71% of academic libraries had librarians performing these upgrades, and 20% of them had paraprofessionals doing it. This work was performed entirely by professional librarians in community colleges, though only 40% of them reported that librarians did this work. Upgrades were performed by paraprofessionals in 31.82% of colleges with enrollment over 10,000, this percentage falling sharply as student enrollment decreased.

The establishment of local series, uniform title headings and authority records was routinely performed by paraprofessional personnel in 25.71% of academic libraries, and by librarians in 71.43%. In colleges with the less than 2,000 students paraprofessionals never performed this task, and 60% of librarians did. Whereas 38.10% of public colleges had paraprofessionals doing this job, only 7.14% of private colleges did. As many as 93.33% of level 1 and level 2 Carnegie Class research universities had librarians carry out this work; 53.33% had paraprofessionals do it.

The establishment of local names, corporate body, and conference headings and authority records was done by paraprofessionals in 22.86% of academic libraries, and by librarians in 68.57%. Here again, many more public colleges had paraprofessionals do this work than private colleges, 25.71% compared to 3.57%. Roughly 10% of community colleges and 4-year degree granting programs had paraprofessionals performing this kind of work, 25% of MA and PHD level Carnegie Class Institutions, and 53.33% of level 1 and 2 Carnegie Class research universities. While no colleges with less than 2,000 students had paraprofessionals do this work, 71.43% of them had librarians do it.

20% of the libraries in the sample had paraprofessionals attending to the establishment of local subject and geographic headings and authority records. Only 5.56% of colleges with 2,000 and 5,000 students had paraprofessionals do this work, while 25% of those with between 5,000 and 10,000 students, and 40.91% with over 10,000 students did. Only 6.9% of 4-year degree granting colleges and 3.57% of all private colleges had paraprofessionals perform this work. 71.43% of college libraries had professional librarians do this work, including 93.75% of colleges with 5,000 to 10,000 students and 100% of level 1 and level 2 Carnegie Class research universities.

College libraries have lost a mean of 0.35 cataloging support staff within the last five years, some losing as many as 6 staff members, and others gaining as many as 7. The colleges with the largest and smallest student enrollments have lost the most support personnel, those with more than 10,000 students losing a mean of 1.31 workers, and those with less than 2,000 students losing a mean of 0.21. MA and PHD level Carnegie Class institutions and Level 1 and 2 Carnegie Class research universities have lost more than other colleges, with mean losses of 0.96 and 1.04 support staff. Public and private colleges seem to have lost approximately the same number of positions.

Over the last five years, these same libraries have gained a mean of 0.09 professional librarians. Colleges with 5,000 to 10,000 current students, which gained 0.35 support staff over this period of time, also gained a mean of 0.60 professional librarians. While most colleges increased their number of librarians, MA and PHD level Carnegie Class institutions actually lost a mean of 0.25.

52.94% of academic libraries participated in library school student mentoring/internship or recruited existing staff and student workers into the cataloging profession. This was especially true of level 1 and level 2 Carnegie Class research universities, 78.57% of which facilitated such internships and recruiting efforts.

On average, the libraries in the sample anticipated the retirement of 0.50 professional librarians performing cataloging functions within the next five years, with community colleges anticipating the fewest, a mean of 0.10. Academic libraries expected a mean of 0.95 paraprofessional staff retirements and a maximum of 6. The most librarian and paraprofessional retirements were anticipated by colleges with over 10,000 students, with a mean of 0.71 for the former and 1.95 for the latter. Level 1 and level 2 Carnegie Class research universities anticipated an average of 2.46 paraprofessional retirements in the next five years. Public colleges expected more paraprofessional retirements than private ones, a mean of 1.32 to private colleges' 0.42.

2. Salary Issues

73.91% of academic libraries reported that their catalogers had salaries comparable to public service librarians, and an additional 18.84% were unsure. 80% of community colleges claimed their catalogers had comparable salaries. 14.29% of colleges with student enrollments greater than 10,000 reported that their catalogers' salaries were not comparable to that of public service librarians, and there was the most uncertainty in colleges with between 2,000 and 5,000 students, 27.78% of which were unsure of how well their salaries stacked up.

3. Work Rate Compensation

The technical services area tracked turn-around time from acquisitions receipt to cataloging to shelf-ready distribution in 25% of libraries in the sample. 38.46% of 4-year degree granting colleges tracked this information, though only 8.33% of MA and PHD level institutions did so, and no community colleges. Technical service tracking did not vary significantly between public and private colleges or with student enrollment.

Cataloger and staff work product quotas were considered somewhat useful in indicating the quality of cataloging work by 29.23% of academic libraries. 20% said that these quotas were not useful in this regard, 24.22% said that they were misleading, and another 20% reported that the quotas detracted from quality. 42.86% of colleges with 5,000 to 10,000 students said that these quotas detracted from quality, though they were considered more useful in larger colleges, 19.05% of which rated them very useful and 33.33% somewhat useful. 11.11% of community colleges found the quotas very useful quality indicators, whereas 40% of level 1 and level 2 Carnegie Class research universities found them misleading. Public colleges considered the quotas more useful than private colleges, though more than 60% considered them useless, misleading, or harmful to the quality of cataloging work.

55.22% of academic libraries found turn-around time from receipt in cataloging to shelf-ready somewhat useful as an indicator of the quality of cataloging work, and 22.30% found it very useful to this end. This information was considered least useful by colleges with less than 2,000 students, 14.29% of which said that it was not useful, and 17.65% of colleges with between 2,000 and 5,000 students found it misleading. Still, as many as 28.57% of private colleges and 17.95% of public colleges considered turn-around time very useful, including 33.33% of community colleges and 25% of 4-year degree granting programs.

Error rates per bibliographic record were considered very useful or somewhat useful quality indicators by 82.09% of the sample, and none of the libraries felt that they detracted from the quality of cataloging work. As many as 73.33% of MA and PHD level Carnegie Class institutions found error rates per bibliographic record somewhat useful. Another 20% of these institutions found them very useful, and 0% of this group considered them detracting or misleading. 35.71% of colleges with less than 2,000 students and of all private colleges found error rates to be very useful indicators.

47.76% of libraries found the completeness of bibliographic record to be very useful in determining the quality of cataloging work, including 67.86% of 4-year degree granting colleges. None of the libraries in the sample found this information misleading, and only colleges with over 10,000 students said that it detracted from the quality of work. 100% of community colleges considered the completeness of bibliographic record useful to some extent, as did 87.18% of public colleges.

While most libraries considered error rates per authority record a useful quality indicator, 26.23% said it was not at useful at all, and as many as 42.86% of schools with student enrollment between 2,000 and 5,000. 14.29% of these same colleges rated the information very useful, and another 42.86% somewhat useful. 33.33% of community colleges and 26.67% of level 1 and level 2 Carnegie Class research universities considered error rates per authority record very useful.

Over half the libraries surveyed considered error rates per holdings record somewhat useful as a quality measure, and 27.69% considered these rates very useful. The smallest and the largest colleges, those with less than 2,000 and more than 10,000 students, rated this information the most useful, though as many as 64.71% of colleges with 2,000 to 5,000 students enrolled said that it was somewhat useful. 13.33% of level 1 and level 2 Carnegie Class research universities found these error rates misleading, and 5.26% of public colleges, which account for 3.08% of all college libraries in the sample.

Error rates per physical processing were found very useful in indicating the quality of cataloging work by 36% of private colleges, and by 28.13% of academic libraries in total. 75% of colleges with student enrollments between 2,000 and 5,000 considered the error rates per physical processing somewhat useful, and the remainder found them either very useful or not useful at all; none found them detracting or misleading. 33.33% of level 1 and level 2 Carnegie Class research universities did not consider these particular rates useful, and 13.33% of these colleges felt they were misleading.

85.08% of the sample considered patron and staff complaints useful to some extent in evaluating the quality of cataloging work, though 5.97% said these complaints were misleading. These complaints were valued the most by 4-year degree granting colleges, 42.86% of which found them very useful, and by colleges with 5,000 to 10,000 students, 43.75% of which did the same. 12.50% of public colleges reported that this information was not useful, as did 22.22% of community colleges. Nonetheless, most of the college libraries in the sample seemed to believe that patron and staff complaints were at least somewhat useful.

Patron or staff commendations were considered very useful quality indicators by 43.28% of libraries, and somewhat useful 41.79%. Commendations were valued least highly by MA and PHD level Carnegie Class institutions, 20% of which did not find them useful and an additional 6.67% misleading. On the other hand, 50% of level 1 and level 2 Carnegie Class research universities considered commendations very useful, and 93.11% of 4-year degree granting colleges found them useful quality indicators to some degree. As many as 46.15% of public colleges considered commendations very useful, and no academic libraries in the sample believed that they detracted from the quality of cataloging work in any way.

Support and accomplishment of departmental and library goals was considered very useful in determining the quality of cataloging work by 60.61% of the sample, and somewhat useful by 30.30%. Only 9.09% of libraries felt that this was not a useful indicator and none considered it misleading or felt it detracted from the work. 75% of private colleges found it very useful, as did 50% of public colleges. 21.43% of colleges with fewer than 2,000 students did not find it useful, however, the rest found it very or somewhat useful. 100% of level 1 and 2 Carnegie Class research universities found the support and accomplishment of library/departmental goals useful to some extent.

5. Outsourcing

45.71% of academic libraries outsourced authority control in the form of obtaining new and updated authority records. This outsourcing occurred most often in private colleges and in higher level academic institutions, as in level 1 and level 2 Carnegie Class research universities, 73.33% of which had outsourced this work, and MA and PHD level Carnegie Class institutions, 50% of which had. Only 10% of community colleges outsourced the obtaining of new/updated authority records.

Authority control in the form of updating headings in bibliographic records was outsourced by 37.14% of libraries in the sample, including 57.14% of private colleges, and 42.86% of colleges with less than 2,000 current students. Only 10% of community colleges outsourced any of this work, compared to 34.48% of 4-year degree granting colleges, 43.75% of MA and PHD level institutions, and 53.33% of level 1 and level 2 research universities.

The obtaining of new bibliographic records was outsourced by 48.57% of academic libraries, and in as many as 68.18% of those with more than 10,000 students enrolled. 73.33% of level 1 and level 2 Carnegie Class research universities outsourced this kind of bibliographic records work, along with 48.28% of 4-year degree granting colleges. 50% of public colleges outsourced this work, slightly more than the 46.43% of private colleges.

Only 1.43% of academic libraries outsourced item records and inventory services, and these were limited to a very few serving private MA and PHD level colleges with more than 10,000 students enrolled.

22.86% of college libraries outsourced the physical processing/bar-coding of books and materials. These include both public and private colleges, many of them with over 10,000 students, 40.91% of which outsourced this service. Physical processing was outsourced by 25% of MA and PHD level Carnegie Class universities and by 46.67% of level 1 and level 2 Carnegie Class research universities, though by just 10% of community colleges and 13.79% of 4-year degree granting colleges.

The addition of table of contents notes was outsourced by 21.43% of academic libraries in the sample, including an overwhelming number of colleges with more than 10,000 students, 45.45%. Meanwhile, no colleges with between 2,000 and 5,000 students had this work outsourced. This work was also outsourced by 37.5% of MA and PHD level institutions and 40% of level 1 and 2 Carnegie Class research universities, as well as a limited number of other colleges in the sample. 28.57% of public colleges outsourced the addition of table of contents notes, and 10.71% of private colleges.

11.43% of college libraries outsourced the addition of book reviews. Most of these were public colleges; only 3.57% of private colleges did so. The addition of book jackets was outsourced by 25.71% of libraries, including 28.57% of colleges with less than 2,000 students and 36.36% of colleges with more than 10,000. No community colleges outsourced book jacket additions, but 27.59% of 4-year degree granting colleges did, along with 25% of MA and PHD level and 40% of level 1 and 2 Carnegie Class research universities; as many as 35.71% of private colleges outsourced this type of work.

Printed continuing resources were outsourced by 4.29% of academic libraries, all of which were public colleges with over 10,000 students. No MA or PHD level Carnegie Class level institutions outsourced continuing resources, and community colleges had the greatest share of those that did with 10% outsourcing.

E-Journals, on the other hand, were outsourced by 35.71% of academic libraries in the sample, including 37.5% of MA and PHD level Carnegie Class institutions. 66.67% of level 1 and level 2 Carnegie Class research universities outsourced E-Journals, and the tendency was greater in colleges with larger student enrollments, starting with 14.29% of colleges with less than 2,000 students, and peaking at 50% of colleges with more than 10,000 students.

E-books were outsourced by 43.86% of public colleges and 46.43% of private colleges, and by a combined 44.29% of all college libraries in the sample. In general, the outsourcing of E-books increased with the student enrollment and the educational level of the institution, though 57.14% of colleges with less than 2,000 students outsourced E-books, a significantly greater percentage than that of colleges with larger student enrollments. 30% of community colleges outsourced E-books, compared to 66.67% of level 1 and level 2 Carnegie Class research universities.

The outsourcing of AV Formats was carried out by 4.29% of academic libraries, 6.9% of 4-year degree granting colleges and 6.67% of level 1 and 2 Carnegie Class research universities. No community colleges or MA and PHD level institutions outsourced AV formats, nor did any colleges with less than 2,000 students. Other digital formats were outsourced by 5.71% of academic libraries, including 9.52% of public colleges, but no private colleges. Other digital formats were outsourced most by colleges with over 10,000 students, 13.64% of which did so, and by community colleges, 10% of which outsourced these formats.

Foreign language resources were outsourced by 8.57% of academic libraries, and slightly more by those belonging to private colleges. A considerable portion of these were colleges with 5,000 to 10,000 students, 18.75% of which outsourced foreign language resources. 12.5% of MA and PHD level Carnegie Class institutions outsourced these materials, as did 13.33% of level 1 and level 2 Carnegie Class research universities.

2.86% of college libraries outsourced materials in cataloging backlogs, including 7.14% of colleges with less than 2,000 students enrolled. No colleges with between 2,000 and 5,000 students or with more than 10,000 students outsourced materials in their backlogs, nor did any community colleges or MA and PHD level Carnegie Class institutions.

None of the academic libraries in the sample outsourced all of their materials.

42.86% of academic libraries used MarcEdit or another MARC editor to preview records and globally edit to local standards prior to loading. These included 33.33% of public colleges and 57.14% of private colleges. While no community colleges used a MARC editor for this purpose, 60% of level 1 and level 2 Carnegie Class research universities did, along with 48.28% of 4-year degree granting colleges and 43.75% of MA and PHD level Carnegie Class institutions.

31.43% of libraries used local integrated systems to review loaded records and globally edit to local standards whenever possible. Local integrated systems were used least by colleges with more than 10,000 students, of which, 22.73% used them. 43.75% of MA and PHD level and 33.33% of level 1 and 2 Carnegie Class universities utilized local systems for this kind of quality control, but only 10% of community colleges did the same.

21.43% of libraries always spot checked all vendor records, including 37.5% of colleges with 5,000 to 10,000 students, but only 9.09% of those with over 10,000 students. 40% of community colleges did so and more than 25% of 4-year degree granting colleges. Only 6.67% of level 1 and level 2 Carnegie Class research universities always spot checked.

When complete reviews were not possible, 38.57% of academic libraries spot checked vendor records, including 50% of all private colleges and 50% of colleges with fewer than 2,000 students enrolled. While 41.38% of 4-year degree granting colleges, 43.75% of MA and PHD level Carnegie Class institutions, and 46.67% of level 1 and level 2 Carnegie Class research universities spot checked vendor records in these instances, only 10% of community colleges followed suit.

No or minimal reviews of vendor supplied records were performed in 15.71% of academic libraries. These were primarily public colleges, 21.43% of which performed no or minimal review. 27.27% of colleges with over 10,000 students did not perform reviews either, considerably more than in colleges with fewer students enrolled. 96.55% of 4-year degree granting colleges reviewed vendor supplied records to some extent, whereas 30% of community colleges and 25% of MA and PHD level institutions did not.

6. State of Cataloging Education in Library Schools

Many academic libraries felt that recent library hires were poorly prepared in classification systems. 50% reported that their new employees were minimally prepared in this field and 10% said that they were not prepared at all. 16% felt their hires were well prepared. This dissatisfaction was deepest in MA and PHD level Carnegie Class institutions, 20% of which said their hires were not prepared at all in classification systems, and 50% of which said their hires were minimally prepared. Private colleges said that their library hires were less prepared than public colleges; only 36.84% felt that their hires were prepared or well prepared.

22.92% of academic libraries considered their recent hires prepared in subject/genre thesauri systems, and 54.17% found them minimally prepared. Only 8.33% considered these hires well prepared. 41.67% of libraries belonging to colleges with between 2,000 and 5,000 students said their new hires were not at all prepared in this area, and another 41.67% said that they were minimally prepared. Meanwhile, 46.15% of colleges with 5,000 to 10,000 students found their recent hires prepared in this way, and 22.22% of colleges with less than 2,000 students found them well prepared. 83.33% of community colleges reported that their hires were minimally prepared in subject/genre thesauri systems, and 44.44% of MA and PHD level institutions said their hires were not prepared at all.

With regards to classification and subject/genre analysis, principles, rules, and tools, 55.32% of the sample said that recent hires were minimally prepared, and 21.28% not prepared at all. Level 1 and 2 Carnegie Class research universities were the most satisfied with their hires preparedness in this regard, though 66.67% of this group felt that they were minimally prepared. 41.18% of private colleges found their new employees not prepared at all in this area, as compared to 10% of public colleges.

64.44% of libraries in the sample said that their recent hires were completely unprepared in Java and PERL script applications; a meager 2.22% said that their hires were well prepared. 77.78% of 4-year degree granting colleges found recent hires not at all prepared, however, 50% of community colleges found them prepared. Public colleges found their hires less prepared than private colleges did, 67.86% of the former saying hires were not prepared at all and 58.82% of the latter.

When asked about cataloging rules and tools (including descriptive cataloging), 18% of the sample said that recent library hires were well prepared, and another 18% said that they were prepared. 46% of academic libraries considered recent hires minimally prepared in this subject matter. Recent hires in colleges with 5,000 to 10,000 students were considered the most prepared, 38.46% said that they were prepared and 23.08% well prepared. 30.77% of level 1 and level 2 Carnegie Class research universities found their hires well prepared and only 7.69 said they were not prepared at all. As many as 40% of MA and PHD level Carnegie Class institutions considered their recent hires not at all prepared in cataloging rules and tools.

36.17% of academic libraries found their hires prepared when it came to information technology and social behavior in the organizational context. 66.67% of community colleges called their recent hires prepared, and the remaining 33.33% said that they were minimally prepared. 36.84% of 4-year degree granting colleges felt that their hires were not at all prepared in this way. 35.29% of all private colleges felt the same way, none of them considering their hires well prepared in this area.

As many as 82.22% of academic libraries categorized recent hires as not at all prepared or minimally prepared in metadata standards for digital resources like Dublin Core, MODS, VRA, Open Archives Initiative, etc.. 17.78% of libraries considered their hires prepared and none considered them well prepared. 75% of colleges with 2,000 to 5,000 students enrolled said that their hires were not at all prepared in this area, much more than in colleges with smaller and larger enrollments. Community colleges were the least satisfied with recent hires skills in this area, 60% calling them not at all prepared, as compared to 22.22% of MA and PHD level institutions and 25% of level 1 and 2 research universities.

Only 15.56% of libraries in the sample considered recent hires prepared in abstracting and indexing and none considered them well prepared. 48.89% of academic libraries considered their recent hires not at all prepared in this area. Colleges with 5,000 to 10,000 students and those with more than 10,000 found recent hires slightly better prepared than colleges with smaller enrollments, 58.33% of those with over 10,000 students considering hires minimally prepared, as opposed to 8.33% of colleges with between 2,000 and 5,000 students. Level 1 and level 2 Carnegie Class research universities were also more satisfied with their hires' aptitude in this area, 36.36% categorizing them as prepared and another 36.36% as minimally prepared.

In terms of the electronic delivery of services, 28.26% of academic libraries considered recent hires prepared and 41.3% minimally prepared. 50% of level 1 and 2 Carnegie

Class research universities said their hires were prepared in the electronic delivery of services, significantly more than the 26.32% of 4-year degree granting colleges and 0% of MA and PHD level institutions. 38.89% of private colleges found hires not prepared at all in this way, though 5.56% found them well prepared.

34.7% of academic libraries were satisfied with the preparedness of recent hires in the field of technical services, categorizing them as prepared or well prepared, with an additional 42.86% categorizing them as minimally prepared. While 46.15% of colleges with 2,000 to 5,000 students said their hires were completely unprepared in technical services, 35.71% of colleges with 5,000 to 10,000 students considered them prepared, and 22.22% of colleges with fewer than 2,000 students considered them well prepared. 28.57% of community colleges called their hires well prepared in this area, as did 16.67% of level 1 and level 2 Carnegie Class research universities, and the same percentage of all public colleges in the sample.

40.43% of academic libraries reported that recent library hires were not at all prepared in web and local network system administration and management, including 69.23% of colleges with between 2,000 and 5,000 students. 57.14% of colleges with more than 10,000 students enrolled said their hires were minimally prepared in this area. Community colleges were in an even split, 50% saying their hires were prepared and the other 50% saying they were not at all prepared. Public colleges had a slightly higher opinion of their hires skills in this area than private colleges, 27.59% categorizing them as prepared and 34.48% as minimally prepared.

While 26.32% of private colleges considered their recent hires completely unprepared in the cataloging of books, only 6.45% of public colleges felt the same way. 54.84% of public colleges said that hires were minimally prepared and 38.71% said that they were prepared or well prepared. In total, 48% of academic libraries considered recent hires minimally prepared, 22% prepared, and 16% well prepared. Colleges with 2,000 to 5,000 students were again the least satisfied, 46.15% claiming hires were not at all prepared to catalog books, and level 1 and level 2 Carnegie Class research universities were the most satisfied, 30.77% saying their hires were well prepared to do so.

When it came to cataloging non-book formats and digital resources, 32.65% of libraries said recent hires were not at all prepared in this area and 44.9% said they were minimally prepared. 6.12% of college libraries considered their hires well prepared in cataloging non-books, including 14.29% of colleges with student enrollments between 5,000 and 10,000 students. 85.71% of community colleges said hires were minimally prepared in this regard, along with approximately 45% of 4-year degree granting colleges and MA and PHD level Carnegie Class institutions.

47.92% of academic libraries categorized new employees as not at all prepared in the cataloging of continuing and integrating resources. 8.33% considered them well prepared and 16.67% considered them prepared, though none of these were community colleges or colleges with 2,000 to 5,000 students; 75% of the latter considered recent hires not at all prepared. Colleges with more than 5,000 students were somewhat more satisfied with new hires' skills in this area, approximately 15% categorizing them as well prepared.

In the cataloging of law materials, 65.22% of libraries considered recent hires completely unprepared and only 10.87% considered them either prepared or well prepared. 100% of colleges with 2,000 to 5,000 students enrolled categorized hires as not at all prepared in this area, as did 77.78% of 4-year degree granting colleges and more than half of all other types of colleges.10.34% of public colleges found recent hires prepared in the cataloging of law materials and none found them well prepared.

15.22% of academic libraries said that their recent hires were prepared in the cataloging of music and 60.87% said that they were not prepared at all. Only 11.76% of private colleges felt their hires were prepared or well prepared in this field, compared to 24.04% of public colleges. 72.22% of 4-year degree granting colleges considered hires not at all prepared, whereas 30.77% of level 1 and level 2 Carnegie Class universities considered them prepared and 7.69% well prepared.

In the cataloging of archives and rare materials, 17.24% of academic libraries belonging to public colleges and 11.11% of those belonging to private colleges considered their recent hires prepared. 53.19% of college libraries in the sample said their hires were completely unprepared, and only 2.13% said they were well prepared. 33.33% of colleges with between 5,000 and 10,000 students considered recent hires prepared in cataloging archives and rare materials. None of the colleges in the sample with 2,000 to 5,000 students categorized recent hires as prepared or well prepared in this area.

2.08% of academic libraries said that their recent hires were well prepared in XML and/or XSLT, and these were limited to level 1 and level 2 Carnegie Class research universities with more than 10,000 students. 33.33% of colleges with less than 2,000 students enrolled considered recent hires prepared in XML and XSLT and the remaining 66.67% considered them completely unprepared. 84.21% of 4-year degree granting colleges said that hires were not at all prepared in this subject matter.

None of the libraries in the sample categorized their recent hires as well prepared in the economics and metrics of information and 57.78% felt that they were not prepared at all. 18.18% of colleges with 2,000 to 5,000 students considered new hires minimally prepared and none considered them prepared, let alone well prepared. 20% of community colleges said that their hires were prepared in this field, while 40% said hires were minimally prepared and another 40% said they were not prepared at all.

23.4% of academic libraries considered recent hires prepared in discovery tools and applications and 43.55% said they were minimally prepared. 42.86% of colleges with more than 10,000 students said that their hires were prepared or well prepared in this area. 31.58% of private colleges called their hires prepared in discovery tools, almost twice as many as public colleges, 50% of which categorized hires as minimally prepared.

33.33% of libraries reported that their recent hires were not at all prepared in authority control, including 55.56% of colleges with less than 2,000 students, but only 7.14% of those with between 2,000 and 5,000. 64.29% of the latter considered hires minimally prepared, as did 57.14% of colleges with over 10,000 students. Broken out by type of college, MA and PHD level institutions and level 1 and level 2 research universities were the most satisfied with their hires' skills in this area, over 30% of each categorizing them as prepared or well prepared. 50% of private colleges felt hires were not prepared at all in this area, while 56.67% of public colleges said they were minimally prepared.

Recent library hires seemed prepared to an extent in the fields of web usability, user research, and human interface design. 33.33% of the sample said their hires were minimally prepared in these areas, and 39.58% said they were prepared. 4.17% even said they were well prepared. 57.14% of community colleges said that their hires were prepared and the remaining 42.86% minimally prepared. 44.44% of MA and PHD level Carnegie Class institutions and 36.84% of 4-year degree granting colleges reported that their new hires were prepared in these areas, and 46.67% of all public colleges.

When it came to international MARC bibliographic, authority and holding standards, 18.37% of the sample considered recent hires prepared, 14.29% considered them well prepared, and 42.86% considered them minimally prepared. 50% of colleges with over 5,000 students categorized their hires as prepared in this field; thought 58.33% of those with between 2,000 and 5,000 said they were not at all prepared. 44.44% of MA and PHD level Carnegie Class institutions said their hires were prepared and another 44.44% of the same institutions said they were not prepared at all. 85.71% of community colleges considered their hires minimally prepared in these standards. 50% of private colleges said that recent hires were not at all prepared, as opposed to 9.68% of public colleges.

51.06% of academic libraries considered new library employees not at all prepared in data modeling, warehousing, and mining. None of the libraries in the sample said recent hires were well prepared in these areas and 14.89% said that they were prepared. 63.16% of 4-year degree granting colleges categorized recent hires as not prepared at all and just 10.53% categorized them as prepared. Community colleges were split evenly between not prepared at all, minimally prepared, and prepared.

As many as 82.85% of academic libraries considered their recent hires minimally or not at all prepared in information systems analysis. 25% of colleges with 2,000 to 5,000 students currently enrolled considered recent hires prepared in information systems analysis, more than colleges with smaller and larger enrollments, even while 50% of these colleges characterized their new hires as not at all prepared in this field. Community colleges were the most satisfied with the preparedness of recent hires, 50% considering them prepared and 19.67% minimally prepared.

While 14.89% of college libraries said that recent hires were prepared in programming languages and applications, 63.83% reported that they were not prepared at all. Only 5.26% of 4-year degree granting colleges considered recent hires prepared in this area, 78.95% of these colleges reporting that they were unprepared. Community colleges were slightly more satisfied, 33.33% of which categorized recent hires as prepared in programming languages and applications and 16.67% of which categorized them as minimally prepared. 13.79% of public colleges and 16.67% of private colleges considered recent hires prepared in this field.

In terms of relational database design, 58.33% of academic libraries in the sample considered recent hires not prepared at all and 25% considered them minimally prepared. 58.33% of colleges with between 2,000 and 5,000 students said their hires were unprepared in relational database design. These percentages were greater in colleges with less than 2,000 or more than 10,000 students. 57.14% of community colleges said new hires were prepared in this area, as compared to Level 1 and level 2 Carnegie Class research universities, 76.92% of which said they were not prepared at all.

29.17% of academic libraries reported that recent hires were prepared in OCLC systems and services and an additional 6.25% that they were well prepared. Colleges with between 5,000 and 10,000 students considered their hires the most prepared, 38.46% of which said they were prepared and 46.15% minimally prepared. 50% of community colleges considered hires prepared and none considered them completely unprepared. 35% of 4-year degree granting colleges and 33.33% of MA and PHD level Carnegie Class institutions felt otherwise.

Just 6.25% of academic libraries felt that recent library hires were well prepared in digital libraries and collections, though 27.08% categorized them as prepared and 41.67% as minimally prepared. A quarter of the sample felt that recent hires were not at all prepared in this area, including 44.44% of colleges with less than 2,000 students, 41.67% of colleges with between 2,000 and 5,000, and 50% of all private colleges. Generally, colleges with larger student enrollments were more satisfied with their new employees' performance in this area; only 7.69% of college with 5,000 to 10,000 students considered their hires unprepared and 46.15% considered them prepared. As many as 71.43% of community colleges found their recent hires prepared in digital libraries and collections and 14.29% found them well prepared.

26.09% of college libraries considered recent hires prepared in experiential learning practicum, whereas 43.48% considered them minimally prepared and 21.74% not prepared at all. 20% of community colleges found their recent hires well prepared in this area, along with 11.11% of MA and PHD level Carnegie Class institutions and smaller percentages of 4-year degree granting colleges and level 1 and 2 Carnegie Class research universities. Nonetheless, 33.33% of colleges with 2,000 to 5,000 students considered new hires not at all prepared in this area, as did 38.89% of all private colleges.

Most academic libraries considered recent hires prepared in information storage, retrieval, and architecture to some extent. 43.48% of the sample said that new hires were minimally prepared in this area, while 23.92% said they were prepared, and 30.43% said they were not prepared at all. 45.45% of colleges with 5,000 to 10,000 students and 50% of colleges with over 10,000 students considered recent hires minimally prepared. 100% of community colleges felt that recent hires were prepared in information storage, retrieval, and architecture; even as 42.11% of 4-year degree granting colleges said they were completely unprepared. Private colleges overwhelming felt that hires were minimally or not all prepared in this area, with just 11.11% saying they were prepared and 5.56% well prepared. Public colleges fared better, 32.14% of which said their recent hires were prepared in these areas.

44.9% of libraries in the sample reported that their recent library hires were prepared in social networking and information. An additional 26.53% said they were minimally prepared and 12.24% well prepared. Recent hires were considered most prepared in colleges with the largest student enrollment, 15.38% of colleges with between 5,000 and 10,000 students and 20% of those with more than 10,000 students said that recent hires were well prepared in social networking and information. No colleges with less than 2,000 students said their new personnel were well prepared in this way and 44.44% of these colleges said that they were minimally prepared. 57.14% of community colleges said that hires were prepared and as many as 28.57% said they were well prepared.

In terms of electronic publishing and scholarly communication, 31.25% of libraries considered their recent hires prepared and 43.75% minimally prepared. 8.33% of colleges with 2,000 to 5,000 students considered their hires well prepared and 41.67% not at all prepared. 71.43% of community colleges said that their hires were prepared in electronic publishing and scholarly communication, significantly more than other types of colleges. 41.11% more public colleges than private ones categorized recent hires as prepared, and no private colleges said that they were well prepared.

In principles of historical and contemporary bibliographic control, 40.43% of academic libraries considered recent hires not at all prepared, including 58.33% of colleges with 2,000 to 5,000 students and 50% of those with over 10,000. Most community colleges, MA and PHD level Carnegie Class institutions, and level 1 and level 2 research universities felt that new hires were prepared in these principles to some degree, while more than half of 4-year degree granting colleges said they were not at all prepared.

1. Personnel Issues

At your institution, what basic responsibilities and job requirements are listed in a cataloger's job description?

1. No cataloging job description. No full-time cataloging position.

2. All cataloging, authority control, deleting records, maintaining catalog, plus some reference & instruction.

3. Copy cataloging, some original cataloging, problem solving, and processing books.

4. Cataloging and classifying material, acting as liaison between department/branch we catalog for and cataloging dept., participate in faculty governance, participate in service and research, keep current in area of responsibility and in librarianship.

5. Original and Copy Cataloging of a wide variety of materials in all formats; authority control of names.

6. Cataloging new book acquisitions; creates metadata for various digital projects; supervises student workers; basic system troubleshooting. BA/BS or its equivalent in training or work experience.

7. Responsibilities are cataloging and classifying print and electronic materials in all formats and subjects. Requirements are ALA-accredited MLS or foreign equivalent; knowledge of and experience with LCSH, LCC, AACR2 (soon to be RDA), OCLC; knowledge of and experience with online integrated library systems; skills with networked information resources; knowledge and interest in microcomputer applications in cataloging and related areas; strength in written and oral communication; ability to work independently and cooperatively; willingness to accept new responsibilities.

8. Entering of non shelf-ready new items/upgrading of existing records as needed. Classification of non shelf-ready items.

9. Complex copy & original AACR2/RDA/MARC cataloging, subject analysis, classification, etc., electronic resource management (knowledgebase management, access troubleshooting for E-journals, etc.), synchronization between catalog & ERMS, electronic theses & dissertations, authority control (problem resolution post vendor-outsourcing), database maintenance. Support staff (Bachelor's required) are doing all copy and most original cataloging. MLS (with cataloging experience, AACR2, MARC, LCSH, LCC, etc.) is required for the section lead (supervision, workflow management, liaison with other departments, project management, etc.)

10. Masters in Library Science, familiarity with OCLC, Original Cataloging capability.

11. Responsibilities: Original and complex Copy Cataloging of all formats, authority control, supervision, record maintenance, management of programs/processes, liaison with cataloging vendors, committee work. Requirements: ALA-Accredited MLS, knowledge of authority control, experience with OCLC or other utility, ability to work with a variety of computer programs, ability to work with languages other than English.

12. Creation of MARC records for all forms of material through derived and original cataloguing. All cataloguers have additional responsibilities e.g. public service, link checker, authority work, etc. Copy Cataloging, sending workform/item to Raleigh for when original cataloging is needed.

13. Original or Copy Cataloging of all materials in all formats into ILS.

14. Oversee all cataloging responsibilities, both for print, serial, and e-books; maintain quality control within the OPAC; maintain communication with other departments regarding availability of materials.

15. Knowledge of MARC, AACR2, LC classification, LCSH, MeSH, NLM classification varies with job classification level.

16. Technical Services - all technical services from server maintenance to all cataloguing.

17. Original Cataloging, complex Copy Cataloging, upgrading/enhancing/enriching OCLC master records, authority control, name authority creation.

18. Original & Copy Cataloging.

19. Copy cataloging, Original Cataloging, database maintenance, authority work, keeping stats, writing reports, supervising.

20. My duties include: Original Cataloging and complex Copy Cataloging of materials in all formats; authority work as needed; responsibility for departmental budget; providing cataloging statistics for library director for annual report; working with several other librarians to maintain information in our electronic resources management system; alternating with other librarians in serving at the library's Reference Desk.

This is a faculty position so the Catalog Librarian serves on university committees as do other librarians. We have one other professional cataloger who is specifically responsible for cataloging media materials.

21. Cataloging Authority Control Supervising Student Workers Book Repair Reference and Instruction Systems Other duties as needed...

22. Copy cataloging and Original Cataloging, print materials, Statistics, ILS/Database management, departmental committees, student worker supervision, training, hiring, and firing.

23. All aspects of cataloging: Copy Cataloging, materials processing, overseeing student assistants, etc.

24. The supervision of three paraprofessionals in Copy Cataloging. The cataloger is responsible for the cataloging of all audiovisual, rare and archival materials. Assists with Reference. Weeding of the collection with the Acquisitions Librarian.

25. Depends on the level of the cataloger. The paraprofessional does Copy Cataloging, bibliographic maintenance, and authority control. The librarians do Original Cataloging, bib maintenance, and authority control, and handle serials and electronic resources.

26. For support staff & librarian catalogers: Create original MARC records and/or enhance existing copy, for materials in all formats and in a variety of languages, following national cataloging rules & guidelines. The specific formats and/or the languages handled vary by cataloger. Also create authority records for NACO as needed. For librarian catalogers: Answer questions from copy catalogers; provide cataloging training, as needed, to support staff; keep abreast of developments in cataloging guidelines & technology; engage in scholarly activities; participate in professional activities and/or service.

27. Organizes information resources for easy bibliographic retrieval and helps to ensure an accessible database of information; Maintains the knowledge and experience of how information is structured; Assists in maintaining the integrity of the catalog: the accuracy of descriptions, useful access points and referencing, and control of vocabulary and name forms; Performs original cataloging or conversion of materials, including the creation and editing of authority records nationally and locally for assigned subjects in all formats, print and non-print, paper and electronic; Assign subject headings and classification numbers as access points by performing complex subject analysis on each item, according to national standards using Library of Congress and local classification schemes and Library of Congress subject headings; Keeps abreast of technical developments with electronic information and computer networks; Contributes nationally and locally to the field of librarianship generally, cataloging particularly.

28. Copy and Original Cataloging, LC classification, subject analysis, authority control, contribution of NACO authority records, assigned database quality control tasks.

29. Copy and Original Cataloging of all formats and in all languages. Authority control. Database maintenance. Troubleshooting problems with the ILS. Maintain cataloging policies and procedures manual.

30. (1) Responsible for original and complex Copy Cataloging of printed monographs in a variety of languages. (2) Responsible for serials cataloging in a variety of languages and formats. Responsible for holdings statements, title changes, and other maintenance of bibliographic records for serials. (3) Responsible for original and copy cataloging of library resources in a variety of formats, especially electronic resources. (4) Responsible for re-cataloging or reclassifying (Dewey to LC) selected library materials. (5) Participates in on-going authority control, with special emphasis on series authority work. 6. Serves as liaison between Cataloging and Serials Departments. Participates in serials control projects as needed (e.g., MARC holdings conversion). (6) Maintains awareness of current trends in cataloging and serials control. (7) Performs other duties as assigned. (8) Participates in library committees and governance. (9) Serves as a liaison to at least one academic department. (10) Participates in university committees and governance.

31. Cataloging of various formats including e-resources, authority control, item record and holdings. maintenance, policies and procedures, LC classification and LCSH subject analysis, experience with OCLC Connexion, experience with ILS, unit supervision-staff training-staff appraisal, adherence to national standards, database maintenance, oversight of physical processing, quality control of unit work, backlog reduction and management, student worker supervision-training-evaluation, effective unit representation and coordination with other units and areas, administrative paperwork-statistics-student wages-reports, professional development.

32. Cataloging all types of materials, processing materials, catalog maintenance, committee work.

33. Copy cataloger: Perform Copy Cataloging of materials in all formats; compile and report various cataloging statistics. Update serials holdings in OCLC and the local integrated library system. Cataloging Librarian: Maintain the accuracy & usability of the library's online catalog, including overseeing authority control and efficient display of holdings information. Perform copy and original cataloging of materials,

train staff, write procedures, and recommend policies. Maintain cataloging statistics on collections, oversee cataloging projects, and promote efficient cataloging workflow. Oversee Acquisitions & serials control including coordinating workflow, training staff, writing procedures, and recommending policies. Act as backup for the Systems Librarian as needed, assisting with integrated library system upgrades, especially those features related to the online library catalog. Supervise, do evaluations and hiring of Copy cataloging/ILL staff.

34. Provide cataloging expertise for Original Cataloging in all formats; provide leadership for the cataloging department.

35. Cataloging all formats, authority work, local technical support for the online catalog, liaison with consortium for online catalog and next-generation discovery system,   some time dedicated to reference work.

36. Ensure that all Library materials purchased and donated are properly and correctly classified; Ensure that records for all library materials acquired are added to the Library's database; Load MARC records for electronic books and journals as acquired and /or updated; Ensure that records in the catalog database are updated as needed; Add authority records to the database as needed; Ensure that Library holdings are updated in the OCLC database; Train and supervise the cataloging paraprofessional; Maintain files and statistics related to cataloging; Produce monthly and annual statistical reports; Maintain Cataloging Practices & Procedures notebook.

37. Required: Master's Degree in Library and Information Science from an ALA-accredited institution. 3-5 years work experience. Responsible for original as well as complex Copy Cataloging of materials in all formats.

38. Cataloging, Metadata, Authorities. Know cataloging and metadata scheme, hold ALA approved MLS, experience with an ILS & OCLC.

39. All aspects of cataloging, heavy emphasis on Copy Cataloging, minimal original cataloging.

40. (1) Special Collections materials, especially early materials (2) Modern cataloging in all European languages.

41. Basic responsibilities for a cataloging librarian: Original and complex Copy Cataloging of particular format(s); supervision of copy catalogers; faculty responsibilities. Job requirements: MLS; 1-2 years professional or paraprofessional cataloging experience.

42. Supervision. Original cataloging.

43. Cataloging; OPAC and Systems maintenance; Course Reserves; Reporting & Statistics; Archives cataloging.

44. Familiarity with computers. Must have attention to accuracy and be able to work in a production environment.

45. "(1) Create original / edit copy catalog records a. Items for which no record exists (Original Cataloging) b. Items for which only an incomplete record exists (complex Copy Cataloging) c. Non-English language items (2) Monitor and direct the overall cataloging workflow of library materials daily (3) Perform personnel activities such as train, schedule, supervise, direct and evaluate the work of two cataloging staff members (daily) and two students (weekly; indirectly) including performance management tasks (set performance expectations, conduct evaluations, initiate corrective action) (4) Advise and provide referrals to other library staff from both inside and outside the Cataloging and Processing Department on matters regarding monograph cataloging -- interpretation of catalog records, troubleshooting or record enhancement (weekly) (5) Write and update documentation for monograph cataloging processes (monthly) (6) Coordinate the integration of special projects into the regular cataloging workflow as needed (yearly) (7) Coordinate both external and in-house training opportunities for the Cataloging and Processing staff (yearly) d. Subject Specialist Responsibilities (1) Manage subject-specific collection and acquisitions budget for one or more university academic unit(s) as assigned (weekly) (2) Liaison with faculty in assigned academic department(s), promoting library services and collections, in addition to coordinating and providing specialized reference, research and instruction support (weekly) e. Library Service: Participate in library-wide projects and serve on committees, teams and task forces (monthly).

46. Coordinate and participate in performing original, copy and complex cataloging, classification, series, and subject analysis for all formats. Authority control, database maintenance, special projects.

47. Original and Copy Cataloging. Assign LC classification and subject headings. Retrospective conversion. Supervise copy cataloger.

48. Directs all cataloging activities, maintains an accurate and relevant bibliographic database, supervises the Copy Cataloger, and performs Original Cataloging.

49. Catalog materials in all formats using AACR2, MARC, Dublin Core and other metadata schema. Train and manage staff for cataloging projects. Knowledge of MARCEdit and other cataloging tools for cataloging large sets and global updating of bibliographic info. Continual assessment of processes and efficiencies using new technological applications. Create and update documentation and best practices in the technical services department.

50. First, I don't actually have anyone with the job title of cataloger. Below is part of the description for my Manager of Library Operations; she and I are the only librarians in the Department of Collection and Technical Services.

51. Acquiring copy cataloguing for new acquisitions, enhancement of current records, database clean-up, assists in collection development process.

52. Cataloging library materials according to L of C. and ALA Standards and maintaining authority files.

53. If this means the paraprofessional position, the person does Copy Cataloging through OCLC, including assigning call numbers in Dewey (juvenile materials and media) but not in LC; assists with catalog maintenance in III; and trains and supervises students doing physical processing.

54. Catalog original and complex copy in MARC/AACR2. Perform some Dublin Core metadata for UNM's digital repository. Perform name authority work as appropriate.

55. Determining the call no. of item, and putting attributes of item into library automation system, adding spine labels and jacket covers if needed.

56. Catalog legal materials (descriptive and subject) regardless of format. Thorough knowledge of AACR2rev. LCSH, OCLC, Innovative Interfaces. Supervise paraprofessionals. Explain cataloging practices to others. Participate in the larger university libraries' environment and in appropriate professional organizations.

57. Cataloguing. Other duties as needed (e.g., reference, bibliographic instruction). Part time 'cataloger' does Copy Cataloging, Director does occasional authority work

58. Assign call number, Original Cataloging, database management, OPAC maintenance, authority control.

59. Original cataloging, supervising Copy Cataloging, maintenance of online catalog.

60. All tech services including cataloging, systems maintenance and also reference and liaison with assigned departments.

61. We don't have one.

62. Cataloging and reference duties.

63. Required: Master's Degree in Library and Information Science from an ALA-accredited institution 3-5 years work experience Responsible for original as well as complex copy cataloging of materials in all formats, including complicated remotely accessed electronic resources and foreign titles. Oversees training of copy catalogers in cataloging standards. Requires in-depth knowledge of cataloging principles and practices, bibliographic utilities, library automation software, authority control and metadata standards.

If your institution has a metadata librarian/cataloger, what basic responsibilities and job requirements are listed in the job description?

1. N/A

2. None

3. N/A

4. Don't have access to that job description, and it is only metadata and doesn't include cataloging.

5. Cataloging duties outlined above plus responsible for metadata set-up, creation, quality control on all digital initiatives.

6. Creates metadata for various digital projects. BA/BS or its equivalent in training or work experience.

7. Most of the same folks in #5 are doing non-MARC tasks also: institutional repository (Dublin core), manuscripts processing (ead), and digital image cataloging (mods). Support staff (bachelor's required) are doing all of the record creation). MLS (with cataloging experience, XML/XSLT) is required for the section lead (record transformation, supervision, workflow management, liaison with other departments, project management, etc.)

8. Responsibilities: Cataloging electronic resources, batch processing vendor-supplied cataloging, working with systems staff to develop an institutional repository. Requirements: Knowledge of cataloging rules and standards, knowledge of metadata schema and their application, knowledge of database structure.

9. Sets priorities, develops policies and procedures for metadata creation in all formats. Supervises all staff who does record loading, editing and creation. Responsible for collection management, including weeding projects. Responsible for implementation and integration of discovery systems.

10. Do not presently have a metadata librarian.

11. Maintenance of ERM and Link Solver, programming abilities, manipulation of big data sets and global changes.

12. No separate cataloger.

13. We don't have a full-time metadata cataloger. One of the catalogers is responsible for collection marc record creation of digital collections and the collections in finding aids.

14. Do not have one.

15. We do not have a metadata librarian/cataloger. Several librarians share these duties.

16. I would be the closest thing to that, but we have not had the need for such duties yet. I do catalog some important websites into the catalog.

17. We do not have a specific metadata librarian.

18. Original cataloging, Copy Cataloging, creating and editing MARC records, Reference Desk, Website Coordinator.

19. N/A

20. In addition to the cataloger responsibilities above, the metadata librarian also the creation of metadata for digitization projects and manipulates XML data to create MARC records.

21. Have one now but haven't redone job description. Would include knowledge of Dublin Core

22. Position is Rare Books Librarian / Metadata Librarian. Metadata portion is "Responsible for providing metadata and associated authority control, quality control, knowledge of changing metadata standards and other duties associated with the creation and maintenance of data for intellectual access to Colgate University Libraries' digital projects."

23. Metadata application and profile creation for digital collections, coordination of metadata for all digital collections, education of library staff and others in metadata usage, knowledge and use of various cataloging of e-resources, IR, and metadata standards, research into changing landscape of metadata and implications, e-book cataloging, authority control, use of LC classification and LCSH, database maintenance, manager of institutional repository and digitizing of documents/metadata, policies and procedures, experience with OCLC Connexion and CONTENTdm, experience with ILS, experience with IR platform, experience with Dublin Core, experience with MarcEdit, quality control of unit work, backlog reduction and management, student worker supervision-training-evaluation, effective unit representation and coordination with other units and areas, administrative paperwork-statistics-student wages-reports, professional development.

24. N/A

25. Don't have one.

26. N/A

27. Currently do not have a metadata librarian or cataloger.

28. Don't know - he's next door to me.

29. N/A

30. Basic responsibilities: work with Digital Initiatives staff to provide descriptive metadata; cataloging in specialized areas; supervision. Job requirements: same as above; including experience with metadata standards and schemas.

31. Systems and data management.

32. N/A

33. Create, evaluate and manage metadata for projects as needed.

34. N/A

35. N/A

36. Responsible for the workflow of Technical Services. Supervise staff and provide training. Responsible for inventory of books and government documents.

37. We just hired one, but I'm not all that sure what she does.

38. If this refers to the professional cataloger, the librarian does original and complex Copy Cataloging, assigns all call numbers in LC classification, assigns all subject headings using LCSH, does all necessary authority work, and is in charge of catalog maintenance. The person trains the paraprofessional and act as resource person, reads the LCRIs and the Bulletin, and keeps the paraprofessional updated on changes in practice. The librarian attends consortial catalogers meetings.

39. Create metadata for digital projects and crosswalk metadata to multiple UNM discovery tools. Assist with management of UNM's search appliance.

40. Determining the most needed, the most efficient/user-friendly metadata, the most value for the campus of available databases and electronic media.

41. There is only one librarian, who does it all. Little time to work on metadata.

42. None

43. N/A

44. Cataloging and reference data.

List briefly the cataloging and authority tasks, concepts, and cataloging tools used to train catalogers.

1. OCVLC Workshops

2. Arrive full trained, train yourself, or go to a workshop/webinar by ALCTS, etc.

3. OCLC, webinars and seminars through local consortiums and national groups,

4. Copy cataloging on OCLC, Original Cataloging, AACR2, Cataloger's Desktop, and Class Web.

5. Most of our training is done with actual cataloging/metadata work. I write the training documentation based on national standards and best practices then have students do the work and go over it with them.

6. Copy cataloging of OCLC copy records, OCLC BFAS, Catalogers Desktop, classification Web. Authority work is outsourced.

7. LMS (Library Management System), MARC guidance on web.

8. AACR2 (and now RDA), LCSH, LCC, CONSER guidelines, basics in authority control (we outsource most of our authority control), principles of archival description. Most of our training is local variation of documentation from SCCTP or the ALCTS/LC workshops.

9. LC classification, LC subject headings, emerging RDA, etc. if needed.

10. AACR2/LCRI; LCSH, LC classification and manuals; PCC tools for creating authority records for the NACO program, bibliographic records for the BIBCO program, subject tools for creating subject proposals for the SACO program; system-related documentation; Catalogers; Desktop, ClassificationWeb, internal policy and procedure documents.

11. All cataloguers are trained to derive records via Z39.50 and to input original records, including assigning class number and subject headings and doing routine authority work. We do training internally using the tools we use every day: ILS, Classweb, etc.

12. Smart Port, Webinar with the Director of Learning Services Technology in Raleigh, World Cat, SirsiDynix.

13. OCLC cataloging including authority controls checks; LCSH; LCC; Cataloger's Desktop; Innovative Millennium ILS.

14. Cataloger's Desktop; webinars from OCLC or Lyrasis; various modules on the Internet.

15. We use PCC documentation for catalogers who will do original or complex Copy Cataloging.

16. None

17. Concepts and knowledge of AACR2, LCSH, LC classification, MARC bib and auth. formats, OCLC Connexion and local ILS searching, identifying, editing, creating and loading skills.

18. A2, LC Subject headings, Ex Libris, Authorities.

19. Copy and Original Cataloging using MARC, Connexion, LCSH, DDC, Voyager, Catalogers Desktop; Authority work with Backstage Library Works, cleanup.

20. Our department is small so I don't have a training list. We do, however, have a departmental handbook that is used as a reference for catalogers and our copy cataloger.

21. AACR2R, LCSH, LC-classification, Home-made tutorials and guide sheets. [I train student assistants, so I keep it basic at first and build up from there.]

22. MCLS (local regional library collaborative) helps provide classes on MARC21, Copy and Original Cataloging, OCLC connexion use. Usually I work with a new staff member one on one at least once a week and then once a month or as needed to go over original materials and other cataloging questions they might have. I also am available for questions daily. I suggest they subscribe to AUTOCAT and OCLC-CAT discussion lists to get a flavor of the profession.

23. Person to person demonstration and explanations, shadowing.

24. Webinars by OCLC and workshops provided by our local network provider, Keystone Library Network, and online resources of the Library of Congress.

25. We have a bookcase of paper resources such as the LC classification schedules, MARC manuals, etc. We have various websites bookmarked and pay for a subscription to Class Web. We outsource authority control to MARCIVE, and receive weekly and monthly reports from them. We have 2 librarians and one paraprofessional cataloger and we train each other whenever need arises. The librarians attend conferences frequently.

26. For all catalogers: (1) LC's MARC Content Designation training course (2) vLC's Cataloging Concepts: Basic Descriptive Cataloging course (3) Tutorials for Cataloger's Desktop & Classification Web (4) In-house training materials for III Millennium and SkyRiver (5) LC;s Basic Subject Cataloging Using LCSH (6) LC's Fundamentals of Library of Congress Classification (7) LC's Basic Creation of Name & Title Authorities. For serials catalogers, add: (1) SCCTP Basic Serials Cataloging (2) SCCTP Advanced Serials Cataloging (3) SCCTP Electronic Serials Cataloging (4) SCCTP Serials Holdings Special formats catalogers may take additional workshops, such as ones offered by OLAC on video cataloging. After training, a new cataloger's records will be reviewed by a more experienced cataloger until the new cataloger's records meet national standards and follow local practices.

27. Copy cataloging, using national library records for bibliographic and NACO work. Catalogers Desktop with emphasis on AACR2, LCSH, MeSH, LC class, and NLM class. OCLC and our local system, Innovative Interfaces product.

28. OCLC Bib. Formats and Standards; classification Web; AACR2r; MARC21 web site; internal documents.

29. Cataloging: descriptive, subject analysis, classification, MARC encoding. Tools: AACR2, LCRI, CONSER manuals, MARC formats, other stuff in Catalogers' Desktop; LC classification through ClassWeb & printed LCCS, classification & Shelf-listing Manual; Subject analysis through Subject headings manual, Subject Cataloging Training Guide, etc. Authority control: to authorize & collocate access points and to provide links from unused terms in public catalog to used ones. Effect of authority records on bib access points through automatic authority control processing. MARC tagging for authorities. Tools: LC authority files, OCLC authority files, MARC format for authority records, Subject Heading Manual, SACO and NACO participants' manuals, etc.

30. Cataloger's Desktop, LC classification, LCSH, NACO manual, Classification web, AACR2 and LCRI, the 3 Subject Manuals, Media/Music/Serials specific documentation, CONSER, ILS documentation, Dublin Core, OCLC and LC authority files, Connexion client. Tasks, concepts: all authority control/all types, full cataloging, all formats.

31. OCLC tutorials, in-house policy and procedure manual.

32. Tools for training: OCLC & other online webinars, reading & FW'ing relevant cataloging listserv postings, in-house training sessions by cataloging librarian, relevant in-person sessions like OCLC regional user meetings & vendor-sponsored meetings, etc.

33. Millennium, OCLC, LCSH tools such as classification Web.

34. ? - Some training is available through local (state) organizations, Library of Congress training sessions, webinars. We have no formal in house training, and very little economic support for further education.

35. Cataloging handbook; Policies and procedures handbook; OCLC training sessions.

36. We ask for knowledge of basic concepts, we mentor in cataloging, authority, OCLC and other systems use. We provide the cataloger with Cataloger's Desktop, classification Web, RDA Toolkit, and will fund training as needed.

37. Our cataloger has been doing cataloging for 25 years and is mainly self-trained.

38. (1) In-house workbooks (2) personally supervised training on OCLC & local III system (3) Bibliographic Description of Rare Books and other publications of ALA/ACRL/RBMS

38. Resources in Cataloger's Desktop, all national cataloging standards; NACO training supplied by the Library of Congress; OCLC webinars/training. OLAC conferences for media cataloger.

39. As a PCC institution, we train our catalogers how to perform national-level authority work

40. No training provided by the library; liberal budget provided for professional development/outside training

41. We use Catalogers Desktop, Bib formats and standards (Online) for National cataloging information; we have an internal wiki with local cataloging standards and project instructions.

42. ClassWeb, OCLC Connexion, Catalog ILS, Marc format, NACO authority training, metadata content management system

43. ExLibris, Voyager, OCLC, Connexion, client and browser, Processing, WorldCat, Cataloging Partners, books, Processing Amazon orders, AACR2, Catalogers' Desktop, ClassWeb, in-house documentation/policies and procedures.

44. LCSH, DDC, LCCS, LC authorities, MARC, RDA, FRBR.

45. In house documentation with screen shots and video capture--Other Technical Services websites--Webinars--In house training sessions in computer classroom.

46. For training, we use our local consortia, Tampa Bay Library Consortium, TBLC, for formal training in cataloging, both face-to-face and online, provided through TMQ, formerly Marc of Quality (Deborah Fritz); my staff attends as many of those as they can. Some training specific to our LMS provided through FCLA or through ALEPH/ExLibris, and we develop our own in-house documentation and classes. We are using Cataloger's desktop and the RDA toolkit. We use tutorials from OCLC and LYRASIS.

47. ISBD/AACR2 MARC manual/ILS documentation Shelf-listing/Cutter table/Shelf-listing manual Subject heading assignment/LCSH.

48. Basically, a new cataloger is familiarized with the MARC system, the basic nature of cat. Records and authority files, and the ALA rules governing the cataloging process. The trainee is also given copies of the books and finding aids involved.

49. One starts with OCLC, the Bibliographic Formats and Standards, and AACR2. This leads to a discussion of the history of cataloging rules and of the various roles of LC, OCLC, OhioLINK, and our consortium within OhioLINK. The paraprofessional keeps our copy of Dewey and the Cutter table, and has to learn to use it. The professional keeps our copy of AACR2, the LC classification, LCSH, the LCRIs, and the Bulletins, and has the access to Classweb and RDA, and has the responsibility of knowing and interpreting all of those for the paraprofessional.

50. LCRI's, PCC guidelines and documentation.

51. OCLC is valued tool, used to validate correct info in multiple fields for identification, bib and item records.

52. Since this library is a full Program for Cooperative Cataloging participant, all catalogers are trained to the PPC standards for NACO, BIBCO, CONSER AND SACO. We have access to the Cataloger's Desktop.

53. Tools: OCLC and Aleph and their manuals; LC subject heading books, LC classification tables, technical services manual written by the cataloguer for procedures specific to MVCC, various web sites as listed here: http://mvcc.libguides.com/aecontent.php?pid=107821&sid=810946 Whenever I get a new part-time cataloguer, I start with the basics, as if they've never had a cataloguing course before. (My current part-time librarian cataloguer did not.) My "student" gets written exercises to do for everything I teach them. I take them through how to look at an item from a cataloguing standpoint, then identify on the item what information is important for cataloguing. I introduce them to LC classification and subject headings. I then introduce them to MARC and AACR2. They then learn where the information from the item to be catalogued fits into the MARC record and in the proper format. Next is the intro to OCLC and Aleph and how to navigate through them. I focus on books first, and give them practice items to first catalogue on MARC worksheets. Once this is mastered, I introduce them to copy cataloguing. Eventually, when they have mastered cataloguing books, I introduce them to AV and other types of items as well as original cataloguing.

54. Proper matching of OCLC records, concept of authority control.

55. Explanation of Marc fields, Dewey classification, LC heading, match new to subject heading and location to what already own, WorldCat, each call number is unique.

56. None

57. Dewey, LC subject headings, OCLC training.

58. Books

Table 1.1:   Is Original Cataloging routinely done by Paraprofessional Support Staff?

	Yes	No
Entire Sample	31.43%	68.57%

Table 1.2:   Is Original Cataloging routinely done by Paraprofessional Support Staff? Broken Out by FTE Student Enrollment

Student Enrollment	Yes	No
Less than 2,000	7.14%	92.86%
2,000 to 5,000	16.67%	83.33%
5,000 to 10,000	37.50%	62.50%
Over 10,000	54.55%	45.45%

Table 1.3:   Is Original Cataloging routinely done by Paraprofessional Support Staff? Broken Out by Type of College

Type of College	Yes	No
Community College	10.00%	90.00%
4-Year Degree Granting College	20.69%	79.31%
MA or PHD Level Carnegie Class Institution	37.50%	62.50%
Level 1 or Level 2 Carnegie Class Research University	60.00%	40.00%

Table 1.4:   Is Original Cataloging routinely done by Paraprofessional Support Staff? Broken Out by Public or Private Status

Public or Private Status	Yes	No
Public	38.10%	61.90%
Private	21.43%	78.57%

Table 1.5:   Is Original Cataloging routinely done by Professional Librarians?

	Yes	No
Entire Sample	88.57%	11.43%

Table 1.6:   Is Original Cataloging routinely done by Professional Librarians? Broken Out by FTE Student Enrollment

Student Enrollment	Yes	No
Less than 2,000	100.00%	0.00%
2,000 to 5,000	83.33%	16.67%
5,000 to 10,000	100.00%	0.00%
Over 10,000	77.27%	22.73%

Table 1.7:   Is Original Cataloging routinely done by Professional Librarians? Broken Out by Type of College

Type of College	Yes	No
Community College	90.00%	10.00%
4-Year Degree Granting College	93.10%	6.90%
MA or PHD Level Carnegie Class Institution	75.00%	25.00%
Level 1 or Level 2 Carnegie Class Research University	93.33%	6.67%

Table 1.8:   Is Original Cataloging routinely done by Professional Librarians? Broken Out by Public or Private Status

Public or Private Status	Yes	No
Public	85.71%	14.29%
Private	92.86%	7.14%

Table 1.9:   Is Copy Cataloging routinely done by Paraprofessional Support Staff?

	Yes	No
Entire Sample	81.43%	18.57%

Table 1.10:   Is Copy Cataloging routinely done by Paraprofessional Support Staff? Broken out by FTE Student Enrollment

Student Enrollment	Yes	No
Less than 2,000	64.29%	35.71%
2,000 to 5,000	77.78%	22.22%
5,000 to 10,000	93.75%	6.25%
Over 10,000	86.36%	13.64%

Table 1.11:   Is Copy Cataloging routinely done by Paraprofessional Support Staff? Broken out by Type of College

Type of College	Yes	No
Community College	50.00%	50.00%
4-Year Degree Granting College	79.31%	20.69%
MA or PHD Level Carnegie Class Institution	87.50%	12.50%
Level 1 or Level 2 Carnegie Class Research University	100.00%	0.00%

Table 1.12:   Is Copy Cataloging routinely done by Paraprofessional Support Staff? Broken Out by Public or Private Status

Public or Private Status	Yes	No
Public	83.33%	16.67%
Private	78.57%	21.43%

Table 1.13:   Is Copy Cataloging routinely done by Professional Librarians?

	Yes	No
Entire Sample	58.57%	41.43%

Table 1.14:   Is Copy Cataloging routinely done by Professional Librarians? Broken Out by FTE Student Enrollment

Student Enrollment	Yes	No
Less than 2,000	71.43%	28.57%
2,000 to 5,000	61.11%	38.89%
5,000 to 10,000	50.00%	50.00%
Over 10,000	54.55%	45.45%

Table 1.15:   Is Copy Cataloging routinely done by Professional Librarians? Broken Out by Type of College

Type of College	Yes	No
Community College	70.00%	30.00%
4-Year Degree Granting College	58.62%	41.38%
MA or PHD Level Carnegie Class Institution	50.00%	50.00%
Level 1 or Level 2 Carnegie Class Research University	60.00%	40.00%

Table 1.16:   Is Copy Cataloging routinely done by Professional Librarians? Broken Out by Public or Private Status

Public or Private Status	Yes	No
Public	57.14%	42.86%
Private	60.71%	39.29%

Table 1.17:   Is Name Authority Cooperative work (NACO) routinely done by Paraprofessional Support Staff?

	Yes	No
Entire Sample	11.43%	88.57%

Table 1.18:   Is Name Authority Cooperative work (NACO) routinely done by Paraprofessional Support Staff? Broken Out by FTE Student Enrollment

Student Enrollment	Yes	No
Less than 2,000	0.00%	100.00%
2,000 to 5,000	0.00%	100.00%
5,000 to 10,000	6.25%	93.75%
Over 10,000	31.82%	68.18%

Table 1.19:   Is Name Authority Cooperative work (NACO) routinely done by Paraprofessional Support Staff? Broken Out by Type of College

Type of College	Yes	No
Community College	10.00%	90.00%
4-Year Degree Granting College	0.00%	100.00%
MA or PHD Level Carnegie Class Institution	12.50%	87.50%
Level 1 or Level 2 Carnegie Class Research University	33.33%	66.67%

Table 1.20:   Is Name Authority Cooperative work (NACO) routinely done by Paraprofessional Support Staff? Broken Out by Public or Private Status

Public or Private Status	Yes	No
Public	19.05%	80.95%
Private	0.00%	100.00%

Table 1.21:   Is Name Authority Cooperative work (NACO) routinely done by Professional Librarians?

	Yes	No
Entire Sample	45.71%	54.29%

Table 1.22:   Is Name Authority Cooperative work (NACO) routinely done by Professional Librarians? Broken Out by FTE Student Enrollment

Student Enrollment	Yes	No
Less than 2,000	42.86%	57.14%
2,000 to 5,000	38.89%	61.11%
5,000 to 10,000	37.50%	62.50%
Over 10,000	59.09%	40.91%

Table 1.23: Is Name Authority Cooperative work (NACO) routinely done by Professional Librarians? Broken Out by Type of College

Type of College	Yes	No
Community College	30.00%	70.00%
4-Year Degree Granting College	37.93%	62.07%
MA or PHD Level Carnegie Class Institution	37.50%	62.50%
Level 1 or Level 2 Carnegie Class Research University	80.00%	20.00%

Table 1.24: Is Name Authority Cooperative work (NACO) routinely done by Professional Librarians? Broken Out by Public or Private Status

Public or Private Status	Yes	No
Public	50.00%	50.00%
Private	39.29%	60.71%

Table 1.25: Is Subject Authority Cooperative Work (SACO) routinely done by Paraprofessional Support Staff?

	Yes	No
Entire Sample	11.43%	88.57%

Table 1.26: Is Subject Authority Cooperative Work (SACO) routinely done by Paraprofessional Support Staff? Broken Out by FTE Student Enrollment

Student Enrollment	Yes	No
Less than 2,000	0.00%	100.00%
2,000 to 5,000	0.00%	100.00%
5,000 to 10,000	12.50%	87.50%
Over 10,000	27.27%	72.73%

Table 1.27: Is Subject Authority Cooperative Work (SACO) routinely done by Paraprofessional Support Staff? Broken Out by Type of College

Type of College	Yes	No
Community College	10.00%	90.00%
4-Year Degree Granting College	0.00%	100.00%
MA or PHD Level Carnegie Class Institution	18.75%	81.25%
Level 1 or Level 2 Carnegie Class Research University	26.67%	73.33%

Table 1.28: Is Subject Authority Cooperative Work (SACO) routinely done by Paraprofessional Support Staff? Broken Out by Public or Private Status

Public or Private Status	Yes	No
Public	16.67%	83.33%
Private	3.57%	96.43%

Table 1.29: Is Subject Authority Cooperative Work (SACO) routinely done by Professional Librarians?

	Yes	No
Entire Sample	32.86%	67.14%

Table 1.30: Is Subject Authority Cooperative Work (SACO) routinely done by Professional Librarians? Broken Out by FTE Student Enrollment

Student Enrollment	Yes	No
Less than 2,000	35.71%	64.29%
2,000 to 5,000	38.89%	61.11%
5,000 to 10,000	31.25%	68.75%
Over 10,000	27.27%	72.73%

Table 1.31: Is Subject Authority Cooperative Work (SACO) routinely done by Professional Librarians? Broken Out by Type of College

Type of College	Yes	No
Community College	30.00%	70.00%
4-Year Degree Granting College	24.14%	75.86%
MA or PHD Level Carnegie Class Institution	31.25%	68.75%
Level 1 or Level 2 Carnegie Class Research University	53.33%	46.67%

Table 1.32: Is Subject Authority Cooperative Work (SACO) routinely done by Professional Librarians? Broken Out by Public or Private Status

Public or Private Status	Yes	No
Public	35.71%	64.29%
Private	28.57%	71.43%

Table 1.33: Is Master bibliographic record enhancement in OCLC routinely done by Paraprofessional Support Staff?

	Yes	No
Entire Sample	30.00%	70.00%

Table 1.34:   Is Master bibliographic record enhancement in OCLC routinely done by Paraprofessional Support Staff? Broken Out by FTE Student Enrollment

Student Enrollment	Yes	No
Less than 2,000	7.14%	92.86%
2,000 to 5,000	27.78%	72.22%
5,000 to 10,000	31.25%	68.75%
Over 10,000	45.45%	54.55%

Table 1.35:   Is Master bibliographic record enhancement in OCLC routinely done by Paraprofessional Support Staff? Broken Out by Type of College

Type of College	Yes	No
Community College	0.00%	100.00%
4-Year Degree Granting College	27.59%	72.41%
MA or PHD Level Carnegie Class Institution	43.75%	56.25%
Level 1 or Level 2 Carnegie Class Research University	40.00%	60.00%

Table 1.36:   Is Master bibliographic record enhancement in OCLC routinely done by Paraprofessional Support Staff? Broken Out by Public or Private Status

Public or Private Status	Yes	No
Public	30.95%	69.05%
Private	28.57%	71.43%

Table 1.37:   Is Master bibliographic record enhancement in OCLC routinely done by Professional Librarians?

	Yes	No
Entire Sample	75.71%	24.29%

Table 1.38:   Is Master bibliographic record enhancement in OCLC routinely done by Professional Librarians? Broken Out by FTE Student Enrollment

Student Enrollment	Yes	No
Less than 2,000	85.71%	14.29%
2,000 to 5,000	66.67%	33.33%
5,000 to 10,000	81.25%	18.75%
Over 10,000	72.73%	27.27%

Table 1.39:   Is Master bibliographic record enhancement in OCLC routinely done by Professional Librarians? Broken Out by Type of College

Type of College	Yes	No
Community College	40.00%	60.00%
4-Year Degree Granting College	79.31%	20.69%
MA or PHD Level Carnegie Class Institution	75.00%	25.00%
Level 1 or Level 2 Carnegie Class Research University	93.33%	6.67%

Table 1.40:   Is Master bibliographic record enhancement in OCLC routinely done by Professional Librarians? Broken Out by Public or Private Status

Public or Private Status	Yes	No
Public	66.67%	33.33%
Private	89.29%	10.71%

Table 1.41:   Is participation in PCC, CONSER and BIBCO 1 bibliographic record work routinely done by Paraprofessional Support Staff?

	Yes	No
Entire Sample	10.00%	90.00%

Table 1.42:   Is participation in PCC, CONSER and BIBCO 1 bibliographic record work routinely done by Paraprofessional Support Staff? Broken Out by FTE Student Enrollment

Student Enrollment	Yes	No
Less than 2,000	7.14%	92.86%
2,000 to 5,000	5.56%	94.44%
5,000 to 10,000	6.25%	93.75%
Over 10,000	18.18%	81.82%

Table 1.43:   Is participation in PCC, CONSER and BIBCO 1 bibliographic record work routinely done by Paraprofessional Support Staff? Broken Out by Type of College

Type of College	Yes	No
Community College	0.00%	100.00%
4-Year Degree Granting College	3.45%	96.55%
MA or PHD Level Carnegie Class Institution	12.50%	87.50%
Level 1 or Level 2 Carnegie Class Research University	26.67%	73.33%

Table 1.44:   Is participation in PCC, CONSER and BIBCO 1 bibliographic record work routinely done by Paraprofessional Support Staff? Broken Out by Public or Private Status

Public or Private Status	Yes	No
Public	14.29%	85.71%
Private	3.57%	96.43%

Table 1.45:   Is participation in PCC, CONSER and BIBCO 1 bibliographic record work routinely done by Professional Librarians?

	Yes	No
Entire Sample	22.86%	77.14%

Table 1.46:   Is participation in PCC, CONSER and BIBCO 1 bibliographic record work routinely done by Professional Librarians? Broken Out by FTE Student Enrollment

Student Enrollment	Yes	No
Less than 2,000	21.43%	78.57%
2,000 to 5,000	5.56%	94.44%
5,000 to 10,000	31.25%	68.75%
Over 10,000	31.82%	68.18%

Table 1.47:   Is participation in PCC, CONSER and BIBCO 1 bibliographic record work routinely done by Professional Librarians? Broken Out by Type of College

Type of College	Yes	No
Community College	30.00%	70.00%
4-Year Degree Granting College	6.90%	93.10%
MA or PHD Level Carnegie Class Institution	25.00%	75.00%
Level 1 or Level 2 Carnegie Class Research University	46.67%	53.33%

Table 1.48:   Is participation in PCC, CONSER and BIBCO 1 bibliographic record work routinely done by Professional Librarians? Broken Out by Public or Private Status

Public or Private Status	Yes	No
Public	30.95%	69.05%
Private	10.71%	89.29%

Table 1.49:   Is Master bibliographic record enrichment (adding call numbers, subjects, tables of contents) in OCLC routinely done by Paraprofessional Support Staff?

	Yes	No
Entire Sample	32.86%	67.14%

Table 1.50:   Is Master bibliographic record enrichment (adding call numbers, subjects, tables of contents) in OCLC routinely done by Paraprofessional Support Staff? Broken Out by FTE Student Enrollment

Student Enrollment	Yes	No
Less than 2,000	21.43%	78.57%
2,000 to 5,000	33.33%	66.67%
5,000 to 10,000	25.00%	75.00%
Over 10,000	45.45%	54.55%

Table 1.51:   Is Master bibliographic record enrichment (adding call numbers, subjects, tables of contents) in OCLC routinely done by Paraprofessional Support Staff? Broken Out by Type of College

Type of College	Yes	No
Community College	10.00%	90.00%
4-Year Degree Granting College	34.48%	65.52%
MA or PHD Level Carnegie Class Institution	43.75%	56.25%
Level 1 or Level 2 Carnegie Class Research University	33.33%	66.67%

Table 1.52:   Is Master bibliographic record enrichment (adding call numbers, subjects, tables of contents) in OCLC routinely done by Paraprofessional Support Staff? Broken Out by Public or Private Status

Public or Private Status	Yes	No
Public	30.95%	69.05%
Private	35.71%	64.29%

Table 1.53:   Is Master bibliographic record enrichment (adding call numbers, subjects, tables of contents) in OCLC routinely done by Professional Librarians?

	Yes	No
Entire Sample	67.14%	32.86%

Table 1.54:   Is Master bibliographic record enrichment (adding call numbers, subjects, tables of contents) in OCLC routinely done by Professional Librarians? Broken Out by FTE Student Enrollment

Student Enrollment	Yes	No
Less than 2,000	85.71%	14.29%
2,000 to 5,000	66.67%	33.33%
5,000 to 10,000	68.75%	31.25%
Over 10,000	54.55%	45.45%

Table 1.55:   Is Master bibliographic record enrichment (adding call numbers, subjects, tables of contents) in OCLC routinely done by Professional Librarians? Broken Out by Type of College

Type of College	Yes	No
Community College	40.00%	60.00%
4-Year Degree Granting College	75.86%	24.14%
MA or PHD Level Carnegie Class Institution	68.75%	31.25%
Level 1 or Level 2 Carnegie Class Research University	66.67%	33.33%

Table 1.56:   Is Master bibliographic record enrichment (adding call numbers, subjects, tables of contents) in OCLC routinely done by Professional Librarians? Broken Out by Public or Private Status

Public or Private Status	Yes	No
Public	59.52%	40.48%
Private	78.57%	21.43%

Table 1.57:   Is Subject analysis and subject heading application routinely done by Paraprofessional Support Staff?

	Yes	No
Entire Sample	38.57%	61.43%

Table 1.58:   Is Subject analysis and subject heading application routinely done by Paraprofessional Support Staff? Broken Out by FTE Student Enrollment

Student Enrollment	Yes	No
Less than 2,000	21.43%	78.57%
2,000 to 5,000	33.33%	66.67%
5,000 to 10,000	50.00%	50.00%
Over 10,000	45.45%	54.55%

Table 1.59:   Is Subject analysis and subject heading application routinely done by Paraprofessional Support Staff? Broken Out by Type of College

Type of College	Yes	No
Community College	10.00%	90.00%
4-Year Degree Granting College	34.48%	65.52%
MA or PHD Level Carnegie Class Institution	43.75%	56.25%
Level 1 or Level 2 Carnegie Class Research University	60.00%	40.00%

Table 1.60:   Is Subject analysis and subject heading application routinely done by Paraprofessional Support Staff? Broken Out by Public or Private Status

Public or Private Status	Yes	No
Public	33.33%	66.67%
Private	46.43%	53.57%

Table 1.61:   Is Subject analysis and subject heading application routinely done by Professional Librarians?

	Yes	No
Entire Sample	81.43%	18.57%

Table 1.62:   Is Subject analysis and subject heading application routinely done by Professional Librarians? Broken Out by FTE Student Enrollment

Student Enrollment	Yes	No
Less than 2,000	92.86%	7.14%
2,000 to 5,000	83.33%	16.67%
5,000 to 10,000	87.50%	12.50%
Over 10,000	68.18%	31.82%

Table 1.63:   Is Subject analysis and subject heading application routinely done by Professional Librarians? Broken Out by Type of College

Type of College	Yes	No
Community College	70.00%	30.00%
4-Year Degree Granting College	86.21%	13.79%
MA or PHD Level Carnegie Class Institution	68.75%	31.25%
Level 1 or Level 2 Carnegie Class Research University	93.33%	6.67%

Table 1.64: Is Subject analysis and subject heading application routinely done by Professional Librarians? Broken Out by Public or Private Status

Public or Private Status	Yes	No
Public	76.19%	23.81%
Private	89.29%	10.71%

Table 1.65: Is Classification routinely done by Paraprofessional Support Staff?

	Yes	No
Entire Sample	44.29%	55.71%

Table 1.66: Is Classification routinely done by Paraprofessional Support Staff? Broken Out by FTE Student Enrollment

Student Enrollment	Yes	No
Less than 2,000	35.71%	64.29%
2,000 to 5,000	38.89%	61.11%
5,000 to 10,000	43.75%	56.25%
Over 10,000	54.55%	45.45%

Table 1.67: Is Classification routinely done by Paraprofessional Support Staff? Broken Out by Type of College

Type of College	Yes	No
Community College	20.00%	80.00%
4-Year Degree Granting College	41.38%	58.62%
MA or PHD Level Carnegie Class Institution	37.50%	62.50%
Level 1 or Level 2 Carnegie Class Research University	73.33%	26.67%

Table 1.68: Is Classification routinely done by Paraprofessional Support Staff? Broken Out by Public or Private Status

Public or Private Status	Yes	No
Public	42.86%	57.14%
Private	46.43%	53.57%

Table 1.69: Is Classification routinely done by Professional Librarians?

	Yes	No
Entire Sample	88.57%	11.43%

Table 1.70:   Is Classification routinely done by Professional Librarians? Broken Out by FTE Student Enrollment

Student Enrollment	Yes	No
Less than 2,000	100.00%	0.00%
2,000 to 5,000	94.44%	5.56%
5,000 to 10,000	93.75%	6.25%
Over 10,000	72.73%	27.27%

Table 1.71:   Is Classification routinely done by Professional Librarians? Broken Out by Type of College

Type of College	Yes	No
Community College	100.00%	0.00%
4-Year Degree Granting College	96.55%	3.45%
MA or PHD Level Carnegie Class Institution	62.50%	37.50%
Level 1 or Level 2 Carnegie Class Research University	93.33%	6.67%

Table 1.72:   Is Classification routinely done by Professional Librarians? Broken Out by Public or Private Status

Public or Private Status	Yes	No
Public	88.10%	11.90%
Private	89.29%	10.71%

Table 1.73:   Are Master bibliographic record upgrades in OCLC routinely done by Paraprofessional Support Staff?

	Yes	No
Entire Sample	20.00%	80.00%

Table 1.74:   Are Master bibliographic record upgrades in OCLC routinely done by Paraprofessional Support Staff? Broken Out by FTE Student Enrollment

Student Enrollment	Yes	No
Less than 2,000	7.14%	92.86%
2,000 to 5,000	16.67%	83.33%
5,000 to 10,000	18.75%	81.25%
Over 10,000	31.82%	68.18%

Table 1.75:   Are Master bibliographic record upgrades in OCLC routinely done by Paraprofessional Support Staff? Broken Out by Type of College

Type of College	Yes	No
Community College	0.00%	100.00%
4-Year Degree Granting College	13.79%	86.21%
MA or PHD Level Carnegie Class Institution	37.50%	62.50%
Level 1 or Level 2 Carnegie Class Research University	26.67%	73.33%

Table 1.76:   Are Master bibliographic record upgrades in OCLC routinely done by Paraprofessional Support Staff? Broken Out by Public or Private Status

Public or Private Status	Yes	No
Public	19.05%	80.95%
Private	21.43%	78.57%

Table 1.77:   Are Master bibliographic record upgrades in OCLC routinely done by Professional Librarians?

	Yes	No
Entire Sample	65.71%	34.29%

Table 1.78:   Are Master bibliographic record upgrades in OCLC routinely done by Professional Librarians? Broken Out by FTE Student Enrollment

Student Enrollment	Yes	No
Less than 2,000	57.14%	42.86%
2,000 to 5,000	61.11%	38.89%
5,000 to 10,000	81.25%	18.75%
Over 10,000	63.64%	36.36%

Table 1.79:   Are Master bibliographic record upgrades in OCLC routinely done by Professional Librarians? Broken Out by Type of College

Type of College	Yes	No
Community College	40.00%	60.00%
4-Year Degree Granting College	68.97%	31.03%
MA or PHD Level Carnegie Class Institution	68.75%	31.25%
Level 1 or Level 2 Carnegie Class Research University	73.33%	26.67%

Table 1.80:   Are Master bibliographic record upgrades in OCLC routinely done by Professional Librarians? Broken Out by Public or Private Status

Public or Private Status	Yes	No
Public	64.29%	35.71%
Private	67.86%	32.14%

Table 1.81:   Is Establishment of local series, uniform title headings and authority records routinely done by Paraprofessional Support Staff?

	Yes	No
Entire Sample	25.71%	74.29%

Table 1.82:   Is Establishment of local series, uniform title headings and authority records routinely done by Paraprofessional Support Staff? Broken Out by FTE Student Enrollment

Student Enrollment	Yes	No
Less than 2,000	0.00%	100.00%
2,000 to 5,000	11.11%	88.89%
5,000 to 10,000	25.00%	75.00%
Over 10,000	54.55%	45.45%

Table 1.83:   Is Establishment of local series, uniform title headings and authority records routinely done by Paraprofessional Support Staff? Broken Out by Type of College

Type of College	Yes	No
Community College	10.00%	90.00%
4-Year Degree Granting College	13.79%	86.21%
MA or PHD Level Carnegie Class Institution	25.00%	75.00%
Level 1 or Level 2 Carnegie Class Research University	60.00%	40.00%

Table 1.84:   Is Establishment of local series, uniform title headings and authority records routinely done by Paraprofessional Support Staff? Broken Out by Public or Private Status

Public or Private Status	Yes	No
Public	38.10%	61.90%
Private	7.14%	92.86%

Table 1.85: Is Establishment of local series, uniform title headings and authority records routinely done by Professional Librarians?

	Yes	No
Entire Sample	71.43%	28.57%

Table 1.86: Is Establishment of local series, uniform title headings and authority records routinely done by Professional Librarians? Broken Out by FTE Student Enrollment

Student Enrollment	Yes	No
Less than 2,000	71.43%	28.57%
2,000 to 5,000	72.22%	27.78%
5,000 to 10,000	87.50%	12.50%
Over 10,000	59.09%	40.91%

Table 1.87: Is Establishment of local series, uniform title headings and authority records routinely done by Professional Librarians? Broken Out by Type of College

Type of College	Yes	No
Community College	60.00%	40.00%
4-Year Degree Granting College	75.86%	24.14%
MA or PHD Level Carnegie Class Institution	50.00%	50.00%
Level 1 or Level 2 Carnegie Class Research University	93.33%	6.67%

Table 1.88: Is Establishment of local series, uniform title headings and authority records routinely done by Professional Librarians? Broken Out by Public or Private Status

Public or Private Status	Yes	No
Public	69.05%	30.95%
Private	75.00%	25.00%

Table 1.89: Is Establishment of local name, corporate body, and conference headings and authority records routinely done by Paraprofessional Support Staff?

	Yes	No
Entire Sample	22.86%	77.14%

Table 1.90:   Is Establishment of local name, corporate body, and conference headings and authority records routinely done by Paraprofessional Support Staff? Broken Out by FTE Student Enrollment

Student Enrollment	Yes	No
Less than 2,000	0.00%	100.00%
2,000 to 5,000	5.56%	94.44%
5,000 to 10,000	25.00%	75.00%
Over 10,000	50.00%	50.00%

Table 1.91:   Is Establishment of local name, corporate body, and conference headings and authority records routinely done by Paraprofessional Support Staff? Broken Out by Type of College

Type of College	Yes	No
Community College	10.00%	90.00%
4-Year Degree Granting College	10.34%	89.66%
MA or PHD Level Carnegie Class Institution	25.00%	75.00%
Level 1 or Level 2 Carnegie Class Research University	53.33%	46.67%

Table 1.92:   Is Establishment of local name, corporate body, and conference headings and authority records routinely done by Paraprofessional Support Staff? Broken Out by Public or Private Status

Public or Private Status	Yes	No
Public	35.71%	64.29%
Private	3.57%	96.43%

Table 1.93:   Is Establishment of local name, corporate body, and conference headings and authority records routinely done by Professional Librarians?

	Yes	No
Entire Sample	68.57%	31.43%

Table 1.94:   Is Establishment of local name, corporate body, and conference headings and authority records routinely done by Professional Librarians? Broken Out by FTE Student Enrollment

Student Enrollment	Yes	No
Less than 2,000	71.43%	28.57%
2,000 to 5,000	66.67%	33.33%
5,000 to 10,000	87.50%	12.50%
Over 10,000	54.55%	45.45%

Table 1.95:   Is Establishment of local name, corporate body, and conference headings and authority records routinely done by Professional Librarians? Broken Out by Type of College

Type of College	Yes	No
Community College	60.00%	40.00%
4-Year Degree Granting College	72.41%	27.59%
MA or PHD Level Carnegie Class Institution	43.75%	56.25%
Level 1 or Level 2 Carnegie Class Research University	93.33%	6.67%

Table 1.96:   Is Establishment of local name, corporate body, and conference headings and authority records routinely done by Professional Librarians? Broken Out by Public or Private Status

Public or Private Status	Yes	No
Public	66.67%	33.33%
Private	71.43%	28.57%

Table 1.97:   Is Establishment of local subject and geographic headings and authority records routinely done by Paraprofessional Support Staff?

	Yes	No
Entire Sample	20.00%	80.00%

Table 1.98:   Is Establishment of local subject and geographic headings and authority records routinely done by Paraprofessional Support Staff? Broken Out by FTE Student Enrollment

Student Enrollment	Yes	No
Less than 2,000	0.00%	100.00%
2,000 to 5,000	5.56%	94.44%
5,000 to 10,000	25.00%	75.00%
Over 10,000	40.91%	59.09%

Table 1.99:   Is Establishment of local subject and geographic headings and authority records routinely done by Paraprofessional Support Staff? Broken Out by Type of College

Type of College	Yes	No
Community College	10.00%	90.00%
4-Year Degree Granting College	6.90%	93.10%
MA or PHD Level Carnegie Class Institution	25.00%	75.00%
Level 1 or Level 2 Carnegie Class	46.67%	53.33%

Research University		

Table 1.100:   Is Establishment of local subject and geographic headings and authority records routinely done by Paraprofessional Support Staff? Broken Out by Public or Private Status

Public or Private Status	Yes	No
Public	30.95%	69.05%
Private	3.57%	96.43%

Table 1.101:   Is Establishment of local subject and geographic headings and authority records routinely done by Professional Librarians?

	Yes	No
Entire Sample	71.43%	28.57%

Table 1.102:   Is Establishment of local subject and geographic headings and authority records routinely done by Professional Librarians? Broken Out by FTE Student Enrollment

Student Enrollment	Yes	No
Less than 2,000	64.29%	35.71%
2,000 to 5,000	66.67%	33.33%
5,000 to 10,000	93.75%	6.25%
Over 10,000	63.64%	36.36%

Table 1.103:   Is Establishment of local subject and geographic headings and authority records routinely done by Professional Librarians? Broken Out by Type of College

Type of College	Yes	No
Community College	70.00%	30.00%
4-Year Degree Granting College	72.41%	27.59%
MA or PHD Level Carnegie Class Institution	43.75%	56.25%
Level 1 or Level 2 Carnegie Class Research University	100.00%	0.00%

Table 1.104:   Is Establishment of local subject and geographic headings and authority records routinely done by Professional Librarians? Broken Out by Public or Private Status

Public or Private Status	Yes	No
Public	73.81%	26.19%
Private	67.86%	32.14%

Table 1.105:   How many positions in cataloging library support staff has your agency gained or lost in the past five years?

	Mean	Median	Minimum	Maximum
Entire Sample	-0.35	0.00	-6.00	7.00

Table 1.106:   How many positions in cataloging library support staff has your agency gained or lost in the past five years? Broken Out by FTE Student Enrollment

Student Enrollment	Mean	Median	Minimum	Maximum
Less than 2,000	-0.21	0.00	-3.00	1.00
2,000 to 5,000	0.03	0.00	-2.00	1.50
5,000 to 10,000	0.35	0.00	-3.00	7.00
Over 10,000	-1.31	-1.50	-6.00	3.00

Table 1.107:   How many positions in cataloging library support staff has your agency gained or lost in the past five years? Broken Out by Type of College

Type of College	Mean	Median	Minimum	Maximum
Community College	0.20	0.00	0.00	1.00
4-Year Degree Granting College	0.06	0.00	-2.00	7.00
MA or PHD Level Carnegie Class Institution	-0.96	0.00	-6.00	1.50
Level 1 or Level 2 Carnegie Class Research University	-1.04	-0.50	-6.00	3.00

Table 1.108:   How many positions in cataloging library support staff has your agency gained or lost in the past five years? Broken Out by Public or Private Status

Public or Private Status	Mean	Median	Minimum	Maximum
Public	-0.34	0.00	-6.00	7.00
Private	-0.36	0.00	-6.00	1.50

Table 1.109:   How many positions for professional librarians in cataloging functions has your agency gained or lost in the past five years?

	Mean	Median	Minimum	Maximum
Entire Sample	0.09	0.00	-2.00	2.50

Table 1.110: How many positions for professional librarians in cataloging functions has your agency gained or lost in the past five years? Broken Out by FTE Student Enrollment

Student Enrollment	Mean	Median	Minimum	Maximum
Less than 2,000	0.11	0.00	-1.00	2.00
2,000 to 5,000	-0.15	0.00	-1.50	0.00
5,000 to 10,000	0.60	0.00	0.00	2.00
Over 10,000	-0.10	0.00	-2.00	2.50

Table 1.111: How many positions for professional librarians in cataloging functions has your agency gained or lost in the past five years? Broken Out by Type of College

Type of College	Mean	Median	Minimum	Maximum
Community College	0.20	0.00	0.00	1.00
4-Year Degree Granting College	0.13	0.00	-1.00	2.00
MA or PHD Level Carnegie Class Institution	-0.25	0.00	-2.00	1.00
Level 1 or Level 2 Carnegie Class Research University	0.27	0.00	-2.00	2.50

Table 1.112: How many positions for professional librarians in cataloging functions has your agency gained or lost in the past five years? Broken Out by Public or Private Status

Public or Private Status	Mean	Median	Minimum	Maximum
Public	0.06	0.00	-2.00	2.50
Private	0.13	0.00	-1.00	2.00

Table 1.113: Does your cataloging agency participate in library school student mentoring or internships, or recruiting existing staff and student workers into the cataloging profession?

	Yes	No
Entire Sample	52.94%	47.06%

Table 1.114: Does your cataloging agency participate in library school student mentoring or internships, or recruiting existing staff and student workers into the cataloging profession? Broken Out by FTE Student Enrollment

Student Enrollment	Yes	No
Less than 2,000	42.86%	57.14%
2,000 to 5,000	55.56%	44.44%
5,000 to 10,000	60.00%	40.00%
Over 10,000	52.38%	47.62%

Table 1.115: Does your cataloging agency participate in library school student mentoring or internships, or recruiting existing staff and student workers into the cataloging profession? Broken Out by Type of College

Type of College	Yes	No
Community College	30.00%	70.00%
4-Year Degree Granting College	48.28%	51.72%
MA or PHD Level Carnegie Class Institution	53.33%	46.67%
Level 1 or Level 2 Carnegie Class Research University	78.57%	21.43%

Table 1.116: Does your cataloging agency participate in library school student mentoring or internships, or recruiting existing staff and student workers into the cataloging profession? Broken Out by Public or Private Status

Public or Private Status	Yes	No
Public	51.22%	48.78%
Private	55.56%	44.44%

Table 1.117: Approximately how many of each of the following do you believe will be retiring from your institution within the next five years: Professional Librarians performing mostly cataloging functions?

	Mean	Median	Minimum	Maximum
Entire Sample	0.50	0.00	0.00	3.00

Table 1.118: Approximately how many of each of the following do you believe will be retiring from your institution within the next five years: Professional Librarians performing mostly cataloging functions? Broken Out by FTE Student Enrollment

Student Enrollment	Mean	Median	Minimum	Maximum
Less than 2,000	0.50	0.50	0.00	1.00
2,000 to 5,000	0.28	0.00	0.00	1.00
5,000 to 10,000	0.47	0.00	0.00	2.00
Over 10,000	0.71	1.00	0.00	3.00

Table 1.119: Approximately how many of each of the following do you believe will be retiring from your institution within the next five years: Professional Librarians performing mostly cataloging functions? Broken Out by Type of College

Type of College	Mean	Median	Minimum	Maximum
Community College	0.10	0.00	0.00	1.00
4-Year Degree Granting College	0.53	0.00	0.00	3.00
MA or PHD Level Carnegie Class Institution	0.53	1.00	0.00	1.00
Level 1 or Level 2 Carnegie Class Research University	0.67	0.00	0.00	2.00

Table 1.120: Approximately how many of each of the following do you believe will be retiring from your institution within the next five years: Professional Librarians performing mostly cataloging functions? Broken Out by Public or Private Status

Public or Private Status	Mean	Median	Minimum	Maximum
Public	0.48	0.00	0.00	3.00
Private	0.54	0.50	0.00	2.00

Table 1.121: Approximately how many of each of the following do you believe will be retiring from your institution within the next five years: Library Paraprofessional Support Staff performing mostly cataloging functions?

	Mean	Median	Minimum	Maximum
Entire Sample	0.95	0.00	0.00	6.00

Table 1.122: Approximately how many of each of the following do you believe will be retiring from your institution within the next five years: Library Paraprofessional Support Staff performing mostly cataloging functions? Broken Out by FTE Student Enrollment

Student Enrollment	Mean	Median	Minimum	Maximum
Less than 2,000	0.08	0.00	0.00	1.00
2,000 to 5,000	0.33	0.00	0.00	1.00
5,000 to 10,000	1.18	0.50	0.00	4.50
Over 10,000	1.95	2.00	0.00	6.00

Table 1.123: Approximately how many of each of the following do you believe will be retiring from your institution within the next five years: Library Paraprofessional Support Staff performing mostly cataloging functions? Broken Out by Type of College

Type of College	Mean	Median	Minimum	Maximum
Community College	0.40	0.00	0.00	1.00
4-Year Degree Granting College	0.57	0.00	0.00	4.50
MA or PHD Level Carnegie Class Institution	0.77	1.00	0.00	2.00
Level 1 or Level 2 Carnegie Class Research University	2.46	2.00	0.00	6.00

Table 1.124: Approximately how many of each of the following do you believe will be retiring from your institution within the next five years: Library Paraprofessional Support Staff performing mostly cataloging functions? Broken Out by Public or Private Status

Public or Private Status	Mean	Median	Minimum	Maximum
Public	1.32	1.00	0.00	6.00
Private	0.42	0.00	0.00	4.00

2. Salary Issues

Table 2.1: Do catalogers at your institution have salaries comparable to public service librarians?

	Yes	No	Unsure
Entire Sample	73.91%	7.25%	18.84%

Table 2.2: Do catalogers at your institution have salaries comparable to public service librarians?? Broken Out by FTE Student Enrollment

Student Enrollment	Yes	No	Unsure
Less than 2,000	78.57%	7.14%	14.29%
2,000 to 5,000	66.67%	5.56%	27.78%
5,000 to 10,000	87.50%	0.00%	12.50%
Over 10,000	66.67%	14.29%	19.05%

Table 2.3: Do catalogers at your institution have salaries comparable to public service librarians?? Broken Out by Type of College

Type of College	Yes	No	Unsure
Community College	80.00%	10.00%	10.00%
4-Year Degree Granting College	75.86%	0.00%	24.14%
MA or PHD Level Carnegie Class Institution	73.33%	13.33%	13.33%
Level 1 or Level 2 Carnegie Class Research University	66.67%	13.33%	20.00%

Table 2.4: Do catalogers at your institution have salaries comparable to public service librarians?? Broken Out by Public or Private Status

Public or Private Status	Yes	No	Unsure
Public	75.61%	9.76%	14.63%
Private	71.43%	3.57%	25.00%

3. Work Rate Compensation

Does your cataloging agency have cataloging quotas, and please explain why, or why not.

1. No. Cataloging done on an as-needed basis.
2. No. Just one person who will get it done ASAP, and too many other tasks to make cataloging quotas.
3. No. We are small so as long as there is no backlog, we know work is being done efficiently
4. Not any more.
5. No quotas, we don't have a significant backlog so quotas are meaningless
6. No. We feel artificial goals lead to unnecessary haste and loss of quality.
7. No, because different subject areas and formats require more time to do.
8. No, most of our stock comes in shelf ready so it is a manageable amount and a rough check by eye would tell if work was backlogging. Also one member of staff has other job functions other than cataloguing so cannot dictate the period of time per week to spend on it as it's left up to them to decide.
9. No, we do not do enough original MARC cataloging for quotas and we do not have a backlog of new materials. Targets are set based on projects and based on time (this project should be completed by DATE).
10. No, always try to complete all cataloging as first priority without delay.
11. No quotas. We consider quotas inappropriate for catalogers dedicated to providing high-quality records for the PCC. Each cataloger's job is very fluid and changes from day-to-day, making it impossible to set a number quota.
12. No. The staff is trained and professional and gets the work done. we do not have backlogs. I don't believe in quotas as all cataloguing is not the same and some requires more time, knowledge and effort than others.
13. No, because it is included with the OCLC service or cataloged at the state level.
14. No -- Quality above Quantity -- However, we are pretty well able to keep up with the flow of incoming titles.
15. No - our goal is to provide quality cataloging records that are beneficial for our users; we would like to move our books quicker, but find the records in OCLC are minimal and need updating.
16. No. They are not useful when cataloging staff is so small, that there is nobody to compare it with.
17. No, it's all based on need.
18. Yes, to keep accountability and productivity of cataloging work.
19. No.
20. No. Cataloging is too complex a process and job descriptions to complex to require a quota.
21. No. Instead of setting cataloging quotas; we have worked with other library staff members to establish cataloging priorities. Our highest priority materials are cataloged and processed first. We are also very responsive to requests from library staff and patrons for rush cataloging of urgently needed materials.
22. No, I don't think they are useful and can cause unnecessary stress on staff. We try to have a turn around time of most DLC Copy Cataloging of 3-5 days from receipt to process to shelving.
23. No, only 3-4,000 items cataloged annually--we work to have zero backlogs on a day by day basis.
24. No.
25. No, never. As long as the work is moving through, the supervisor is happy. We do not have any backlogs. We do keep statistics that show individual productivity.
26. Paraprofessional staff has guidelines for how many records they are expected to produce in a year. This guideline is expressed as a range, a minimum acceptable number and a maximum expected number. If they produce above the max expected, they can be awarded a merit pay raise by the university. The librarian catalogers have no quotas or guidelines, although they do need to show that they have produced an acceptable number of records in a year. "Acceptable" is negotiable with the Head of Cataloging.
27. No.
28. No, we have expected turnaround time for most materials to leave the area within 4 weeks of arrival in library
29. Not sure what 'cataloging agency' refers to.
30. No. As the head of monographic cataloging, I am opposed to quotas in general. More specifically, we don't have the turnaround demand or the large influx of materials necessary to establish quotas.

31. Not quotas per say but we have guidelines for the length of time a book can be in the backlog before being cataloged. Guidelines are 3 weeks for items w/ LC copy, 3 months for member/original.

32. Yes, based on numbers of materials in unit backlogs, incoming amounts on average, format requirements, and staff experience in cataloging. The idea is to provide a method to constantly decrease our backlogs, and focus our attention on that. It is also to help us remember that while we do other things, cataloging is our main role.

33. No, there is too much variety in difficulty of cataloging different types of materials to be able to determine a fair quota. We are more concerned about quality.

34. No.

35. No.

36. We do not have quotas. While it is expected that materials will be processed as quickly as possible, there is no specific time limit on how long it should take. Due to cuts in budgets, we also do not get as much as we did 4-5 years ago. Materials needed immediately are identified and rushed through as necessary.

37. No, I am expected to move all items selected through in a 'timely manner', but the volume varies considerably.

38. No.

39. No. Instead we have goals that are written service standards that include: cataloging of materials within three weeks of their receipt, rush requests of received materials are cataloged within one business day.

40. No. Since we have no backlog we just try to keep up.

41. No.

42. Not really - informal (100 items per month).

43. No because we catalog so many types of items and the balance of original or Copy Cataloging is always in flux.

44. No. We do not establish quotas unless there is a cataloging backlog. We do not now have a backlog. We have qualitative measures.

45. No, library director checks for spelling errors only

46. No; we have only one cataloger.

47. Yes. Production is emphasized in the unit. We monitor monthly stats. Numbers are used to justify the positions.

48. No, just have not ever done this.

49. No quotas. Performance is not based on quantity.

50. No, we have acceptable timelines for processing materials.

51. No, not seen as necessary.

52. No we are project based and project driven. Copy cataloging flows so efficiently that we do not have backlogs so no need for quotas. We work on a service model as well as project based so we have service standards books will be cataloged within 72 hours of receipt.

53. No, because we are all cross trained and work across barriers, acquisitions and cataloging and serials management are merged; and we perform and oversee all collection assessment and development as well, so we are too busy.

54. No, not really. Our cataloguer is experienced and dedicated. There has never been need for a quota. 55. We have limited space for a backlog, though, so if there were cataloguing slowdowns, there would be consequences.

56. Never heard of them, although I'm not surprised if they exist elsewhere.

57. No. So far we've been lucky.

58. No -- too much variation in type of cataloging and specializing amongst staff -- multiple formats, foreign languages, etc., to have a standard applicable to all or even most.

59. Not to my knowledge.

60. No. Statistics on cataloging throughput is gathered and assessed regularly. However, no quotas are set due to variations in difficulty of materials being handled.

61. No, but I set my own every day when I come in.

62. No.

63. No quota, based on how much money we have to purchase new.

64. No, cataloger does other library work including a heavy instruction load in September and June.

65. No.

66. No.

Table 3.1:   Does your technical services area track turn-around time from Acquisitions receipt to Cataloging to shelf-ready distribution?

	Yes	No	Don't Know
Entire Sample	25.00%	71.67%	3.33%

Table 3.2:   Does your technical services area track turn-around time from Acquisitions receipt to Cataloging to shelf-ready distribution? Broken Out by FTE Student Enrollment

Student Enrollment	Yes	No	Don't Know
Less than 2,000	25.00%	75.00%	0.00%
2,000 to 5,000	23.53%	76.47%	0.00%
5,000 to 10,000	26.67%	60.00%	13.33%
Over 10,000	25.00%	75.00%	0.00%

Table 3.3:   Does your technical services area track turn-around time from Acquisitions receipt to Cataloging to shelf-ready distribution? Broken Out by Type of College

Type of College	Yes	No	Don't Know
Community College	0.00%	100.00%	0.00%
4-Year Degree Granting College	38.46%	61.54%	0.00%
MA or PHD Level Carnegie Class Institution	8.33%	75.00%	16.67%
Level 1 or Level 2 Carnegie Class Research University	33.33%	66.67%	0.00%

Table 3.4:   Does your technical services area track turn-around time from Acquisitions receipt to Cataloging to shelf-ready distribution? Broken Out by Public or Private Status

Public or Private Status	Yes	No	Don't Know
Public	26.47%	70.59%	2.94%
Private	23.08%	73.08%	3.85%

Does your technical services area track turn-around time from Acquisitions receipt to Cataloging to shelf-ready distribution? Other (please specify)

1. Sometimes.
2. We are in the process of doing this now.
3. Occasionally we do time studies, but not regularly.
4. prompt turn-around is expected and achieved
5. We have attempted to, but not really.
6. We did but are no longer doing so.
7. Generally, our department has an excellent turn around time. Naturally, there are times when new materials are flooding in and materials wait longer to be cataloged.
8. Informally. I keep an eye on carts sitting outside the copy cataloger's desk.
9. Overall yes, but not piece-by-piece.
10. We track cataloging time for books from receipt in cataloging to shelf-ready. We receive and catalog the highest number of materials in books, so this shows our most prevalent turn-around time for the most materials.
11. I don't allow a backlog for items we have ordered. If we get large donations or collections, I set a per-week goal for myself. But no formal tracking.
12. It depends on the material being cataloged.
13. In selected formats.
14. We have at one time, now the large majority of material comes shelf ready and does not go through cataloging.
15. Very informal spot checks.
16. They keep basic statistics, but that's about it. Of course, the employees will fudge the results so they don't look bad.
17. We can but don't. Space constraints ensure that materials are cataloged in a timely fashion.
18. Occasionally.

Table 3.5: How would you rate the use of the following quality indicators in cataloging work: Cataloger or staff work product quotas?

	Very Useful	Somewhat Useful	Not Useful	Misleading	Detracts from Quality
Entire Sample	6.15%	29.23%	20.00%	24.62%	20.00%

Table 3.6: How would you rate the use of the following quality indicators in cataloging work: Cataloger or staff work product quotas? Broken Out by FTE Student Enrollment

Student Enrollment	Very Useful	Somewhat Useful	Not Useful	Misleading	Detracts from Quality
Less than 2,000	0.00%	14.29%	35.71%	35.71%	14.29%
2,000 to 5,000	0.00%	37.50%	18.75%	25.00%	18.75%
5,000 to 10,000	0.00%	28.57%	7.14%	21.43%	42.86%
Over 10,000	19.05%	33.33%	19.05%	19.05%	9.52%

Table 3.7: How would you rate the use of the following quality indicators in cataloging work: Cataloger or staff work product quotas? Broken Out by Type of College

Type of College	Very Useful	Somewhat Useful	Not Useful	Misleading	Detracts from Quality
Community College	11.11%	33.33%	22.22%	22.22%	11.11%
4-Year Degree Granting College	7.41%	29.63%	18.52%	25.93%	18.52%
MA or PHD Level Carnegie Class Institution	7.14%	21.43%	28.57%	7.14%	35.71%
Level 1 or Level 2 Carnegie Class Research University	0.00%	33.33%	13.33%	40.00%	13.33%

Table 3.8: How would you rate the use of the following quality indicators in cataloging work: Cataloger or staff work product quotas? Broken Out by Public or Private Status

Public or Private Status	Very Useful	Somewhat Useful	Not Useful	Misleading	Detracts from Quality
Public	7.89%	31.58%	18.42%	23.68%	18.42%
Private	3.70%	25.93%	22.22%	25.93%	22.22%

Table 3.9: How would you rate the use of the following quality indicators in cataloging work: Turn-around time from receipt in Cataloging to ready for shelf?

	Very Useful	Somewhat Useful	Not Useful	Misleading	Detracts from Quality
Entire Sample	22.39%	55.22%	7.46%	8.96%	5.97%

Table 3.10: How would you rate the use of the following quality indicators in cataloging work: Turn-around time from receipt in Cataloging to ready for shelf? Broken Out by FTE Student Enrollment

Student Enrollment	Very Useful	Somewhat Useful	Not Useful	Misleading	Detracts from Quality
Less than 2,000	21.43%	50.00%	14.29%	7.14%	7.14%
2,000 to 5,000	29.41%	47.06%	0.00%	17.65%	5.88%
5,000 to 10,000	6.67%	60.00%	6.67%	13.33%	13.33%
Over 10,000	28.57%	61.90%	9.52%	0.00%	0.00%

Table 3.11:   How would you rate the use of the following quality indicators in cataloging work: Turn-around time from receipt in Cataloging to ready for shelf? Broken Out by Type of College

Type of College	Very Useful	Somewhat Useful	Not Useful	Misleading	Detracts from Quality
Community College	33.33%	33.33%	11.11%	11.11%	11.11%
4-Year Degree Granting College	25.00%	57.14%	3.57%	10.71%	3.57%
MA or PHD Level Carnegie Class Institution	20.00%	53.33%	13.33%	0.00%	13.33%
Level 1 or Level 2 Carnegie Class Research University	13.33%	66.67%	6.67%	13.33%	0.00%

Table 3.12:   How would you rate the use of the following quality indicators in cataloging work: Turn-around time from receipt in Cataloging to ready for shelf? Broken Out by Public or Private Status

Public or Private Status	Very Useful	Somewhat Useful	Not Useful	Misleading	Detracts from Quality
Public	17.95%	58.97%	10.26%	10.26%	2.56%
Private	28.57%	50.00%	3.57%	7.14%	10.71%

Table 3.13:   How would you rate the use of the following quality indicators in cataloging work: Error rates per bibliographic record?

	Very Useful	Somewhat Useful	Not Useful	Misleading	Detracts from Quality
Entire Sample	25.37%	56.72%	11.94%	5.97%	0.00%

Table 3.14:   How would you rate the use of the following quality indicators in cataloging work: Error rates per bibliographic record? Broken Out by FTE Student Enrollment

Student Enrollment	Very Useful	Somewhat Useful	Not Useful	Misleading	Detracts from Quality
Less than 2,000	35.71%	42.86%	14.29%	7.14%	0.00%
2,000 to 5,000	35.29%	52.94%	11.76%	0.00%	0.00%
5,000 to 10,000	20.00%	66.67%	13.33%	0.00%	0.00%
Over 10,000	14.29%	61.90%	9.52%	14.29%	0.00%

Table 3.15: How would you rate the use of the following quality indicators in cataloging work: Error rates per bibliographic record? Broken Out by Type of College

Type of College	Very Useful	Somewhat Useful	Not Useful	Misleading	Detracts from Quality
Community College	33.33%	44.44%	22.22%	0.00%	0.00%
4-Year Degree Granting College	28.57%	53.57%	14.29%	3.57%	0.00%
MA or PHD Level Carnegie Class Institution	20.00%	73.33%	6.67%	0.00%	0.00%
Level 1 or Level 2 Carnegie Class Research University	20.00%	53.33%	6.67%	20.00%	0.00%

Table 3.16: How would you rate the use of the following quality indicators in cataloging work: Error rates per bibliographic record? Broken Out by Public or Private Status

Public or Private Status	Very Useful	Somewhat Useful	Not Useful	Misleading	Detracts from Quality
Public	17.95%	61.54%	12.82%	7.69%	0.00%
Private	35.71%	50.00%	10.71%	3.57%	0.00%

Table 3.17: How would you rate the use of the following quality indicators in cataloging work: Completeness of bibliographic record?

	Very Useful	Somewhat Useful	Not Useful	Misleading	Detracts from Quality
Entire Sample	47.76%	37.31%	13.43%	0.00%	1.49%

Table 3.18: How would you rate the use of the following quality indicators in cataloging work: Completeness of bibliographic record? Broken Out by FTE Student Enrollment

Student Enrollment	Very Useful	Somewhat Useful	Not Useful	Misleading	Detracts from Quality
Less than 2,000	50.00%	35.71%	14.29%	0.00%	0.00%
2,000 to 5,000	64.71%	23.53%	11.76%	0.00%	0.00%
5,000 to 10,000	40.00%	53.33%	6.67%	0.00%	0.00%
Over 10,000	38.10%	38.10%	19.05%	0.00%	4.76%

Table 3.19: How would you rate the use of the following quality indicators in cataloging work: Completeness of bibliographic record? Broken Out by Type of College

Type of College	Very Useful	Somewhat Useful	Not Useful	Misleading	Detracts from Quality
Community College	33.33%	66.67%	0.00%	0.00%	0.00%
4-Year Degree Granting College	67.86%	17.86%	14.29%	0.00%	0.00%
MA or PHD Level Carnegie Class Institution	40.00%	46.67%	13.33%	0.00%	0.00%
Level 1 or Level 2 Carnegie Class Research University	26.67%	46.67%	20.00%	0.00%	6.67%

Table 3.20: How would you rate the use of the following quality indicators in cataloging work: Completeness of bibliographic record? Broken Out by Public or Private Status

Public or Private Status	Very Useful	Somewhat Useful	Not Useful	Misleading	Detracts from Quality
Public	43.59%	43.59%	10.26%	0.00%	2.56%
Private	53.57%	28.57%	17.86%	0.00%	0.00%

Table 3.21: How would you rate the use of the following quality indicators in cataloging work: Error rates per authority record?

	Very Useful	Somewhat Useful	Not Useful	Misleading	Detracts from Quality
Entire Sample	22.95%	45.90%	26.23%	3.28%	1.64%

Table 3.22: How would you rate the use of the following quality indicators in cataloging work: Error rates per authority record? Broken Out by FTE Student Enrollment

Student Enrollment	Very Useful	Somewhat Useful	Not Useful	Misleading	Detracts from Quality
Less than 2,000	38.46%	30.77%	30.77%	0.00%	0.00%
2,000 to 5,000	14.29%	42.86%	42.86%	0.00%	0.00%
5,000 to 10,000	15.38%	61.54%	15.38%	0.00%	7.69%
Over 10,000	23.81%	47.62%	19.05%	9.52%	0.00%

Table 3.23: How would you rate the use of the following quality indicators in cataloging work: Error rates per authority record? Broken Out by Type of College

Type of College	Very Useful	Somewhat Useful	Not Useful	Misleading	Detracts from Quality
Community College	33.33%	22.22%	33.33%	0.00%	11.11%
4-Year Degree Granting College	20.00%	44.00%	36.00%	0.00%	0.00%
MA or PHD Level Carnegie Class Institution	16.67%	66.67%	16.67%	0.00%	0.00%
Level 1 or Level 2 Carnegie Class Research University	26.67%	46.67%	13.33%	13.33%	0.00%

Table 3.24: How would you rate the use of the following quality indicators in cataloging work: Error rates per authority record? Broken Out by Public or Private Status

Public or Private Status	Very Useful	Somewhat Useful	Not Useful	Misleading	Detracts from Quality
Public	18.42%	50.00%	23.68%	5.26%	2.63%
Private	30.43%	39.13%	30.43%	0.00%	0.00%

Table 3.25: How would you rate the use of the following quality indicators in cataloging work: Error rates per holdings record?

	Very Useful	Somewhat Useful	Not Useful	Misleading	Detracts from Quality
Entire Sample	27.69%	50.77%	16.92%	3.08%	1.54%

Table 3.26: How would you rate the use of the following quality indicators in cataloging work: Error rates per holdings record? Broken Out by FTE Student Enrollment

Student Enrollment	Very Useful	Somewhat Useful	Not Useful	Misleading	Detracts from Quality
Less than 2,000	46.15%	38.46%	15.38%	0.00%	0.00%
2,000 to 5,000	23.53%	64.71%	11.76%	0.00%	0.00%
5,000 to 10,000	14.29%	57.14%	21.43%	0.00%	7.14%
Over 10,000	28.57%	42.86%	19.05%	9.52%	0.00%

Table 3.27:   How would you rate the use of the following quality indicators in cataloging work: Error rates per holdings record? Broken Out by Type of College

Type of College	Very Useful	Somewhat Useful	Not Useful	Misleading	Detracts from Quality
Community College	33.33%	44.44%	22.22%	0.00%	0.00%
4-Year Degree Granting College	30.77%	57.69%	11.54%	0.00%	0.00%
MA or PHD Level Carnegie Class Institution	20.00%	60.00%	13.33%	0.00%	6.67%
Level 1 or Level 2 Carnegie Class Research University	26.67%	33.33%	26.67%	13.33%	0.00%

Table 3.28:   How would you rate the use of the following quality indicators in cataloging work: Error rates per holdings record? Broken Out by Public or Private Status

Public or Private Status	Very Useful	Somewhat Useful	Not Useful	Misleading	Detracts from Quality
Public	21.05%	52.63%	21.05%	5.26%	0.00%
Private	37.04%	48.15%	11.11%	0.00%	3.70%

Table 3.29:   How would you rate the use of the following quality indicators in cataloging work: Error rates per physical processing?

	Very Useful	Somewhat Useful	Not Useful	Misleading	Detracts from Quality
Entire Sample	28.13%	51.56%	17.19%	3.13%	0.00%

Table 3.30:   How would you rate the use of the following quality indicators in cataloging work: Error rates per physical processing? Broken Out by FTE Student Enrollment

Student Enrollment	Very Useful	Somewhat Useful	Not Useful	Misleading	Detracts from Quality
Less than 2,000	30.77%	38.46%	30.77%	0.00%	0.00%
2,000 to 5,000	18.75%	75.00%	6.25%	0.00%	0.00%
5,000 to 10,000	35.71%	57.14%	7.14%	0.00%	0.00%
Over 10,000	28.57%	38.10%	23.81%	9.52%	0.00%

Table 3.31:   How would you rate the use of the following quality indicators in cataloging work: Error rates per physical processing? Broken Out by Type of College

Type of College	Very Useful	Somewhat Useful	Not Useful	Misleading	Detracts from Quality
Community College	33.33%	44.44%	22.22%	0.00%	0.00%
4-Year Degree Granting College	29.63%	59.26%	11.11%	0.00%	0.00%
MA or PHD Level Carnegie Class Institution	23.08%	69.23%	7.69%	0.00%	0.00%
Level 1 or Level 2 Carnegie Class Research University	26.67%	26.67%	33.33%	13.33%	0.00%

Table 3.32:   How would you rate the use of the following quality indicators in cataloging work: Error rates per physical processing? Broken Out by Public or Private Status

Public or Private Status	Very Useful	Somewhat Useful	Not Useful	Misleading	Detracts from Quality
Public	23.08%	53.85%	17.95%	5.13%	0.00%
Private	36.00%	48.00%	16.00%	0.00%	0.00%

Table 3.33:   How would you rate the use of the following quality indicators in cataloging work: Patron or staff complaints?

	Very Useful	Somewhat Useful	Not Useful	Misleading	Detracts from Quality
Entire Sample	34.33%	50.75%	8.96%	5.97%	0.00%

Table 3.34:   How would you rate the use of the following quality indicators in cataloging work: Patron or staff complaints? Broken Out by FTE Student Enrollment

Student Enrollment	Very Useful	Somewhat Useful	Not Useful	Misleading	Detracts from Quality
Less than 2,000	15.38%	69.23%	15.38%	0.00%	0.00%
2,000 to 5,000	35.29%	41.18%	5.88%	17.65%	0.00%
5,000 to 10,000	43.75%	50.00%	6.25%	0.00%	0.00%
Over 10,000	38.10%	47.62%	9.52%	4.76%	0.00%

Table 3.35: How would you rate the use of the following quality indicators in cataloging work: Patron or staff complaints? Broken Out by Type of College

Type of College	Very Useful	Somewhat Useful	Not Useful	Misleading	Detracts from Quality
Community College	33.33%	44.44%	22.22%	0.00%	0.00%
4-Year Degree Granting College	42.86%	46.43%	3.57%	7.14%	0.00%
MA or PHD Level Carnegie Class Institution	20.00%	66.67%	6.67%	6.67%	0.00%
Level 1 or Level 2 Carnegie Class Research University	33.33%	46.67%	13.33%	6.67%	0.00%

Table 3.36: How would you rate the use of the following quality indicators in cataloging work: Patron or staff complaints? Broken Out by Public or Private Status

	Very Useful	Somewhat Useful	Not Useful	Misleading	Detracts from Quality
Public	35.00%	47.50%	12.50%	5.00%	0.00%
Private	33.33%	55.56%	3.70%	7.41%	0.00%

Table 3.37: How would you rate the use of the following quality indicators in cataloging work: Patron or staff commendation?

	Very Useful	Somewhat Useful	Not Useful	Misleading	Detracts from Quality
Entire Sample	43.28%	41.79%	10.45%	4.48%	0.00%

Table 3.38: How would you rate the use of the following quality indicators in cataloging work: Patron or staff commendation? Broken Out by FTE Student Enrollment

Student Enrollment	Very Useful	Somewhat Useful	Not Useful	Misleading	Detracts from Quality
Less than 2,000	21.43%	64.29%	14.29%	0.00%	0.00%
2,000 to 5,000	47.06%	35.29%	5.88%	11.76%	0.00%
5,000 to 10,000	56.25%	37.50%	6.25%	0.00%	0.00%
Over 10,000	45.00%	35.00%	15.00%	5.00%	0.00%

Table 3.39: How would you rate the use of the following quality indicators in cataloging work: Patron or staff commendation? Broken Out by Type of College

Type of College	Very Useful	Somewhat Useful	Not Useful	Misleading	Detracts from Quality
Community College	55.56%	22.22%	22.22%	0.00%	0.00%
4-Year Degree Granting College	48.28%	44.83%	3.45%	3.45%	0.00%
MA or PHD Level Carnegie Class Institution	20.00%	53.33%	20.00%	6.67%	0.00%
Level 1 or Level 2 Carnegie Class Research University	50.00%	35.71%	7.14%	7.14%	0.00%

Table 3.40: How would you rate the use of the following quality indicators in cataloging work: Patron or staff commendation? Broken Out by Public or Private Status

Public or Private Status	Very Useful	Somewhat Useful	Not Useful	Misleading	Detracts from Quality
Public	46.15%	38.46%	12.82%	2.56%	0.00%
Private	39.29%	46.43%	7.14%	7.14%	0.00%

Table 3.41: How would you rate the use of the following quality indicators in cataloging work: Support or accomplishment of departmental or library goal?

	Very Useful	Somewhat Useful	Not Useful	Misleading	Detracts from Quality
Entire Sample	60.61%	30.30%	9.09%	0.00%	0.00%

Table 3.42: How would you rate the use of the following quality indicators in cataloging work: Support or accomplishment of departmental or library goal? Broken Out by FTE Student Enrollment

Student Enrollment	Very Useful	Somewhat Useful	Not Useful	Misleading	Detracts from Quality
Less than 2,000	64.29%	14.29%	21.43%	0.00%	0.00%
2,000 to 5,000	70.59%	17.65%	11.76%	0.00%	0.00%
5,000 to 10,000	40.00%	60.00%	0.00%	0.00%	0.00%
Over 10,000	65.00%	30.00%	5.00%	0.00%	0.00%

Table 3.43: How would you rate the use of the following quality indicators in cataloging work: Support or accomplishment of departmental or library goal? Broken Out by Type of College

Type of College	Very Useful	Somewhat Useful	Not Useful	Misleading	Detracts from Quality
Community College	33.33%	55.56%	11.11%	0.00%	0.00%
4-Year Degree Granting College	64.29%	21.43%	14.29%	0.00%	0.00%
MA or PHD Level Carnegie Class Institution	57.14%	35.71%	7.14%	0.00%	0.00%
Level 1 or Level 2 Carnegie Class Research University	73.33%	26.67%	0.00%	0.00%	0.00%

Table 3.44: How would you rate the use of the following quality indicators in cataloging work: Support or accomplishment of departmental or library goal? Broken Out by Public or Private Status

Public or Private Status	Very Useful	Somewhat Useful	Not Useful	Misleading	Detracts from Quality
Public	50.00%	42.11%	7.89%	0.00%	0.00%
Private	75.00%	14.29%	10.71%	0.00%	0.00%

How does your cataloging department define quality?

1. Absence of errors or complaints.
2. Accuracy/time.
3. Accurate, detailed work done in a timely fashion.
4. Speed in getting something on the shelves.
5. Records that adhere to national standards and best practices, are as complete and detailed as possible, and have extra features requested by Reference.
6. Steady output with few errors.
7. Largely, by the completeness of the bibliographic record and the usability of the catalog.
8. We don't have set criteria, as our stock is largely shelf-ready we have learnt to accept that not everything on our catalogue is 100% "correct".
9. We focus on time-to-shelf over quality and we fix/change anything without question that comes back to us as problematic. When we see trends in what is coming back to us, we set up workflows (or training or documentation) to address. We are currently trying to define measurable ways to assess quality for the users. We are trying to figure out which elements "matter" most so that we can focus resources on quality in those areas.
10. High quality, low error rate, quick turnaround.
11. Quality is providing a catalog record meeting the BIBCO Standard Record requirements as quickly & efficiently as possible, making sure requested items get out to the "shelf" within 24 hours.
12. Efficient, effective and timely provision of access to material acquired.
13. Correctness, consistency, quick turn around time, logical location and search terms.

14. The right and complete record for the item; if the record does not display well for the patron, the Reference Librarians and I work out a way to adjust the record to make it more understandable.

15. Providing a high level bibliographic record for an item in an efficient amount of time

16. Reliable access points to improve discovery. Accurate holdings statement to support reliable linking and ILL services.

17. An appropriate balance between productivity and quality work, taking difficulty of the workload into consideration.

18. Work which is without errors and problems - that makes the rest of the library run smoothly

19. Correct marc tagging, applying AACR2, conforming with LCSH, LC classification, duplication of call numbers, typos, and correct local elements, such as mat types, locations, item types, etc, especially elements related to public display.

20. Speed, accuracy

21. Accurate data and enhanced data (Tables of contents, subject headings, summaries, etc.)

22. Our department is small. We have an excellent system of checks and balances set up. We expect high quality work of ourselves. We expect that work be completed accurately with adequate detail to meet the needs of our patrons in as timely as manner as is possible given our current work load.

23. Getting the records in the catalog with as few errors as possible. Providing detail at access points. Getting the books on the shelf in a timely fashion. [We generally have a very small backlog.]

24. Can a patron find the materials they are looking for by using the catalog? Does the call number lead them to the location where they can find the item? Does the search they use lead them to find helpful materials?

25. Ideally, 24-hour turnaround between departments: 1 day receiving to cataloging, 1 day cataloging to processing, 1 day processing to circulation. Strive for no record errors in essential locating fields (call no., title, author, publisher, subject headings). All processing, bar-coding, and call numbering is double-checked.

26. Quality is 99% accurate. We proofread and make necessary corrections.

27. We control access points in OCLC before exporting the record to our local catalog. We use the weekly and monthly reports from our external authority control vendor to make database corrections. If we see a problem, we discuss it and get "on the same page." We keep up with changes in the field and incorporate those in our daily workflows.

28. A high quality record meets national cataloging standards, is free from significant errors, performs effectively in our ILS & OPAC, and meets patron needs for finding and accessing library resources. A "significant error" is one that impedes FRBR users' tasks or causes the record to index incorrectly in the library catalog.

29. Item accessible after cataloging. Prefer no typos; catch errors in Copy Cataloging; series treatment matches our local decision. We are part of a shared catalog with 3 other campuses using the shared bibliographic record concept. Quality also equals other campuses being able to use our cataloging with no modifications other than local notes.

30. Combination of completeness, timeliness, and lack of errors.

31. Proper coding (both ILS and MARC) is used. There are no mistakes in spelling. Call number is present and correct. Subjects are present and correct. Data in the bib record accurately matches the physical item. Item record is attached and correct. Physical processing is complete and done neatly.

32. Accuracy of data; fullness of data; circulation rates for monographs (currently over 50% within 1st year after cataloging).

33. Quality is a complete I-level, level 3 bibliographic description, done in a timely manner

34. Few, if any, errors in the records or in processing.

35. Dedication to balancing both national cataloging standards and local needs.

36. Providing the best access to materials for our users.

37. There is no set definition.

38. It is not officially defined, but in practical terms we define it as creating accurate and correct bibliographic and item records that comply with MARC/OCLC standards and local standards, application of relevant and useful subject headings, and assignment of correct call numbers (taking local practice into consideration).

39. Access points/metadata that enhances an end-user's experience. Consistency.

40. Complete full description and classification in a timely fashion with >2% error rate.

41. We are a small rural community college that relies heavily on OCLC and Copy Cataloging. The quality of the OCLC records is important to us.

42. Best accuracy possible under the circumstances.

43. A record done to the best of our ability to help in the aid of finding the material.

44. By qualitative measures such as error rate in certain fields in the bibliographic record, defined by local standards for each format.

45. If it meets user needs.

46. Accurate records that support discovery; reasonable turn around time; adherence to consortium standards.

47. Quality facets include: timeliness, completeness, accuracy, free from judgment, using vocabulary familiar to the general public. A quality record enables the user to find it and understand and utilize the description.

48. If no one complains, we are doing a good job.

49. Positive attitude; dedication to job; responsiveness to patrons and fellow employees.

50. Completeness of record. Patron able to retrieve materials.

51. Doing the very best we can in the shortest timeframe and with as few errors as possible.

52. Quality is finishing or completing projects and providing excellent service and information to our users. The Department balances completing projects in a timely manner with providing the best information possible to our users. Constantly asking, what do our users on campus and internationally need and want to discover and need to locate in our libraries?

53. We believe in doing things correctly the first time. I have found that when we push productivity, error rates increase, sometimes dramatically. We want to get our books on the shelves, and we want them correctly classified and cataloged. When we run our new books report, our Library Operations Manager is able to catch most problems in classification and cataloging. We also have fairly high standards re physical processing, both from our vendor and our student assistants. We are running a vastly understaffed department, and we have student assistants doing all kinds of work once done by paraprofessionals, and paraprofessionals doing work once done by librarians.

54. Completeness of record, consistency, turnaround time, communication with the rest of the library, transparency.

55. Work done correctly, and, they hope, quickly. However, in this business it's impossible to satisfactorily achieve both.

56. A full record, free from errors, which contains as much information as possible to assist in retrieval.

57. It is highly (and appropriately) individualized. For example, one cataloger is very productive at more routine work, while another may produce less quantity but deals with specialized materials in foreign languages important to our collections and mission.

58. Doing their level best, I suppose.

59. Handle an item correctly the first time and you will never have to handle it again!

60. Quality cataloguing records contain accurate spelling and are accurately catalogued according to AACR2 rules. They contain summary statements and contents notes to maximize their usefulness to those searching in the online catalog. They should include local subject headings if needed to accommodate the needs of the college's students and faculty. Subject headings should be consistent within the database (authority control). Quality processing is neat and straight.

61. "Our catalog is as good as OCLC's contributors." We cannot improve our catalog because we cannot contribute to OCLC and our consortium overlays bib records so all local modifications are lost.

62. Accuracy, simplicity, and workflow and use of good headings.

63. Complete bibliographic records with contents notes and subject headings.

64. Accurate, neat, timely processing.

65. Don't have a cataloging department.

4. Technology

Please explain any difficulties your area has faced in improving and upgrading staff-use of hardware and software technology.

1. My computer is a Pentium 4 processor and the IT department won't replace it, but I don't think this is what you mean.

2. Our budget is small, so far we have been able to purchase necessary PCs and pay monthly bills to Lyrasis so we are doing ok.

3. We don't have any.

4. Don't know.

5. Mostly cost.

6. Funds have been short and will get shorter soon.

7. There are many things I would love to automate, if we had more technical resources devoted to cataloging efficiency and post-cataloging quality assessment. We have a large technology staff but most of their resources are on the discovery side. Our cataloging tools need workflow efficiency and quality assurance functionality built in.

8. IT Department separate from library staffing.

9. Lack of funds for hardware upgrades means catalogers don't always have the most current hardware. Some catalogers are reluctant to use newer software, citing the time required to become familiar with each program.

10. None.

11. Having time and availability of training that goes beyond the basics

12. Finding opportunities for outside training has been difficult. But getting hardware upgrades has been even more difficult!

13. Being as everyone in our Technical Services dept. retired at the same time, the new people coming in had little experience with our OPAC system (Voyager). Learning it and training staff has been by far the hardest part of dealing with technology in cataloging.

14. With software changes, we are faced with errors that are not the fault of the cataloger but have to be fixed. With the upgrade to Horizon 7.5, we face the issue of new computer not able to read the software; we deal with computers that are now glitchy and often shut down. Horizon sent us a patch that helps but we still face issues.

15. More advanced and detailed training for efficient and effective use of hardware and software.

16. None.

17. We have to learn on our own, mostly, unless we can make use of free webinars. Sometimes it is challenging to find training or to learn on our own.

18. Our most serious challenge recently has been in obtaining adequate support from our vendors to enable us to receive the maximum benefit from our software.

19. Cost is always a factor, so we do as much for free as we possibly can. We are switching to Koha from III. I'm a little concerned that Koha doesn't have as many error catching utilities available, and quality is very important to me.

20. Campus IT upgrade to Windows 7 has caused difficulties with our binding software, possible problems with the barcode scanners Upgrade to new version of OCLC Connexion client resulted in difficulties in locating network drives where bib records are stored.

21. Staff has trouble following standards for holdings records and their input using Ex Libris Voyager. Editing of online catalog requires knowledge of CSS, XML, and other web programming technologies--customization interface desired.

22. When it comes to hardware and software technology we need to use the campus Information Technology Department for updating so it delays implementation.

23. If we catalogers have any problems that we can't resolve, we notify our university's IT department. There is one individual within the university assigned primarily to assist library personnel. He usually fixes any problems within a day or so. We also have a systems librarian who has the primary responsibility for this.

24. Since the library reports under the Vice President for Academic Computing, we have had a robust technology & software budget. However, we did find it impossible to continue to pay the ever-increasing OCLC cataloging costs.

25. None. We are on a three year cycle for replacing computer workstations. Our library IT staff keeps our software up-to-date as we request it. We do have out-of-date work "desks." We purchased that equipment in 1991 for 1991 technology and we are trying to use 21st century computers, including double monitors. Not very adaptable and pretty permanent in where they reside. Wiring to equipment from holes in floor near the work areas which are 4 quadrants to a workspace.

26. None.

27. We are fortunate to have PCs that are able to handle all our needs, and we can generally purchase any software we need. Biggest problems are 'retooling' when applications change radically (e.g., Prism to Connexion).

28. When the windows operating system changes we have problems with our OCLC Connexion macros, shortcut keys, text strings, local toolbars, and some operational problems - it is very typical that some things don't work, and make the client crash, and so on. This also affects our ILS, as well. When our browser software is upgraded, we often lose our bookmarks to cataloging and other things so we have to rebuild. When Cataloger's Desktop or Classification web make upgrades, we sometimes have logon issues. Diacritics can be adversely affected with some software upgrades.

29. N/A

30. Our university IT is sometimes slow in installing new hardware/software. IT is rather resistant to library suggestions. Printing needs of cataloging tasks were not really assessed during last change of printer vendor.

31. Changes to software or procedures in Millennium are often difficult to integrate into the workflow. We have also been hampered by the need to replace some of our hardware, primarily due to costs.

32. Cataloging is done by one professional, myself, and half the time by one (very capable) staff member. Getting any training for new software is nearly impossible. We are self taught. The budget for new hardware has varied over the years, and we in the library have little or no in put or control over what is purchased. The upside, we are not restricted in what we can download or use.

33. Our main difficulty involves support from the university's IT department in terms of upgrading equipment and trouble-shooting. Our automation system is remotely hosted by the vendor, so we have no problems with hardware or software at that end.

34. I am in charge of both the cataloging area and the system area so, no difficulties except costs.

35. We haven't assessed our cataloging workflow in quite some time as we are a small staff and are assigned multiple duties beyond cataloging. We have resisted out sourcing but think that once some of our employees retire it will be something to look at.

36. We haven't had any really other than lack of funds to purchase helps such as Cataloger's Desktop.

37. We are fortunate that we are able to upgrade staff hardware at scheduled times. Software enhancements are usually handled locally by supervisors, or if there are a large number of people who need the training, we can bring in a presenter.

38. Cost, working with IT staff

39. We moved to a new ILS this past year. Cataloging ceased for about 4 months during the transition. New workflow had to be implemented after the transition was complete. All things considered, it went very smoothly.

40. Training, adoption

41. Difficulties are associated with learning curves that are associated with new hardware or software.

42. None

43. Hardware has not been a problem. Lehigh Libraries has a 3 year life cycle replacement of computers and laptops and we try to share and keep up by purchasing new technologies such as e-readers, i-pads, etc. Software, we try to identify new tools and software and buy as we want to test or download trials and test. The Libraries are merged with computing so mobile technologies and new software is always at our fingertips such as Google applications, project management software, and video capture software.

44. The only department with more staffing issues than we have is our Systems and IT department; we have no one in IT focused on the LMS or any of the support software we use, and no one to develop macro applications to make our jobs easier. We get new computers and laptops with no problem, but what we need is adequate IT support for acquisitions and cataloging tasks, and for our LMS

45. With a new library system in June 2011 (OPALS), staff had to be retrained and had to work differently from old system (Horizon).

46. Too much is being added, and computerization if everything is becoming more of a hindrance than a help as this keeps going on and on and . . . .

47. We haven't had any problems that I can think of for the permanent staff, but we continually face conflicts between the university's security measures and our student workers' ability to receive updates to our cataloging software.

48. Adaptive technologies are used so seldom that no one will know how they work; frequently find no one knows how to utilize software packages until they are needed: we do not receive enough training in any software or hardware applications to make any use of it.

49. Our institution provides little financial support for professional staff continuing education and no support for paraprofessional staff. Webinars help, but even they require funding on occasion.

50. No problems. I love to learn about new technologies.

51. Director tries to keep us on even rotation for computers and updates on library system.

52. Difficult when doing many other tasks in addition to cataloging to stay "up to date" on cataloging practices.

53. Some of the MARC records from vendors are not very complete. This is a frustration.

Briefly list and explain what you consider the most useful new technologies (hardware, software, etc.) in cataloging and metadata today, such as wikis, blogs, harvesting software, DSpace for institutional repositories, any OCLC or vendor products or services

1. Discovery-level platform.

2. CONTENTdm for digital content management, OAI-PMH for harvesting, DSpace for institutional repositories, VuFind for next generation discovery layer for online catalog, SerialsSolutions records for keeping track of e-resources.

3. We use ContentDM, DSpace, Artstor and other metadata vehicles for various electronic holdings. They are fine. We hope to find a way to limit the siloization.

4. The recent enhancements to Cataloger's Desktop have been very helpful. My colleague monitors several blogs and forwards information to me that is useful so those are helpful as well.

5. E-Prints for repositories, the availability of e.g.: Web Dewey.

6. MarcEdit, OCLC, Connexion, systems that link disperse datasets together (i.e. we have an ETD workflow that pulls student information out of our student information system into our records, it is awesome!)

7. Traditional and evolving OCLC cataloging database, excepting the confusing state of RDA introduction.

8. Vendor-supplied records for large packages of e-books & e-journals, authority control services which do machine matching, ability to globally update large numbers of records.

9. Online tools e.g. Classweb, RDA.

10. OCLC, Innovative Millennium, and Cataloger's Desktop upgrades have made cataloging life so much easier!

11. Blogs.

12. I think web 2.0 applications are helpful in reference but in cataloguing the most help is OCLC or copy cataloguing to expedite materials.

13. OCLC connexion clients, MS SharePoint as local wikis for procedures and documentation.

14. Cataloger's Desktop, Printers, Labels, Ex Libris products/Upgrades.

15. We have recently purchased an Electronic Resource Management Module from the vendor that provides the software to support our OPAC. We are currently in the process of implementing this module; however I expect it to be of tremendous help when implementation is complete.

16. OCLC Connexion is a fine cataloging tool to use. It has helped improve the quality of our work. My student workers find it easy to use (once they understand MARC).

17. Use of OCLC worldcat cataloging partners (Promptcat) program along with in-house macros has changed our cataloging workflow enormously. Use of open-source software (we switched to Evergreen as our ILS) has also created big changes.

18. AUTOCAT, OCLC Cataloging, ListServ for Cataloging, and PERSNAME for Authority.

19. OCLC: the ability to control headings; MARCIVE authority control; electronic discussion lists such as AUTOCAT, MLA-L, MOUG, OLAC-L, and OCLC-CAT for asking questions and getting answers.

20. For us, the most significant new cataloging technology has been SkyRiver, the new bibliographic utility, which enabled us to significantly cut our cataloging costs. This survey asked if catalogers engaged in "master bibliographic record enrichment in OCLC" I had to answer no, because we do our bibliographic record enrichment and master record enhancement in SkyRiver. Both our paraprofessional and librarian catalogers do both record enrichment and master record enhancement in SkyRiver. Our use of MarcEdit and XSLT has also enabled us to manage bibliographic records in a more cost-effective way. The increasing capacity of vendors to supply catalog records, particularly in non-Roman languages, has enabled us to reduce backlogs.

21. Flat screen monitors for hardware. Wikis, harvesting software, Dspace for our IR, OCLC, Summon discovery tool.

22. Vendor supported authority control, vendor supported serial holdings service/link resolvers, online tools (ClassWeb, Catalogers Desktop), wiki's for documentation, ContentDM and similar products for digital collections, integrated cataloging interfaces (Connexion), real-time submission of NACO authority records, the internet in general for finding cataloging-related information.

23. Nothing really new. I do keep track of updates and trends via listservs. Otherwise, our small department does not have the need of the latest and greatest technologies.

24. How "new"? Still for the most part depend on electronic discussion lists rather than wikis or blogs. We are looking at harvesting software and institutional repositories but don't have them yet. We use ContentDM for digitized library resources, but there hasn't been a lot of interest (at least according to Google Analytics) Google Analytics is the best way we have of measuring use of our various systems, even though it's not designed for this application. More & better ways of seeing what our patrons do with all our stuff would be useful. Many technologies that get a lot of press don't seem to have really good user studies behind them. Do they really help our patrons?

25. DSpace for IR, MarcEdit is wonderful, cataloging blogs of various types for timely info - we haven't tried harvesting software but are looking to do this with our IR in the near future - I think OAI. The VIAF is nifty, as is LC's LCSH on SKOS. OCLC's identity service may be useful.

26. ClassWeb is the best resource for easily consulting LCSH and classification.

27. Webinars, wikis, OCLC metadata harvester for website cataloging, new discovery interfaces for OPACs.

28. Authority control has had big improvements- OCLC's controlled headings, for example. Online tools, like LC's classification Web are very efficient, when we can afford them. I would really love to have Cataloger's Desktop, but there is no money. MarcEdit is a wonderful tool for batch processing on the cheap.

29. MarcEdit, In-house staff wiki (Confluence) for staff policies/procedures/best practices, Google docs (for team projects).

30. Define new. Improvements in ILS systems, OCLC resource sharing, Catalogers Desktop and Class Web online tools...FBRB had potential.

31. We rely heavily on OCLC and our local consortium C/W MARS.

32. Use of Google for additional information about persons/books being cataloged very helpful for Spec. Coll. Names, Catalogers Desktop very helpful , Use Library of Congress online catalog to help determine call and classify numbers or author numbers.

33. LTI- authority vendor to help free up staff time.

34. Flexible ILSs that allow multiple ways of uploading/downloading bibliographic records; flexible report-writing modules; global change capabilities. All of these help us to streamline our work.

35. OCLC Cloud computing.

36. MarcEdit - invaluable for batch processing of changes, especially to vendor records. Blogs & RSS feeders for keeping up on changes ListServs for keeping up on changes.

37. MARC Edit helps making batch changes, also helps crosswalk. Also MARC Report identifies errors and allows for batch correction.

38. Wiki for documentation, ClassWeb, CONTENTdm upgrades are improving the usefulness of the product.

39. WorldCat Cataloging Partners, Catalogers' Desktop, ClassWeb, Connexion client and browser.

40. wikis.

41. MARCEdit, Google documents and wikis, smartsheet (project management software), macro programs to work with our ILS system.

42. DSpace has really taken the pain out of mounting archival collections

43. Best new technologies: Dymo LabelWriter 450 and z39.50. Labeling one at a time eliminates need to match books with a sheet of labels. Z39.50 allows us free copy. We no longer deal with agency. Also, our ILS, OPALS, has some excellent features that enhance user experience of the catalogue.

44. Frankly, most of it is a pain in the behind because it only complicates things.

45. We are definitely not on the cutting edge, closer to way back in the pack, when it comes to wikis, blogs, harvesting software, etc. It's nice to be able to keep Bibliographic Formats open in the background on the computer. I find that ClassWeb is great a lot of the time, but I have to go to the paper classification schedules if I'm trying to do a number for a literary author. The trouble is that, whether we have quotas or not, the pressure for production barely leaves time to keep up with the OCLC cat list. I've given up even on Autocat, and definitely don't have time to look for or follow wikis or blogs. I do like having the tools online, at least when I can find what I need in them with the search tools available.

46. Harvesting and crosswalk tools for repurposing metadata (including repurposing MARC).

47. OCLC has been consistently valuable and useful. I know that blogs are great but who really cares? Ha, sorry, but it's true.

48. Actually, the ability to view full-text e-resources while cataloging them. OCLC's "control headings" and macros for creating authority records save incredible amounts of time.

49. OCLC is fantastic! Having access to the manual online saves me a lot of time.

50. OCLC Connexion, for ease of preparing records to add to OCLC and downloading. We don't do much with metadata at this time.

51. Using OCLC records makes life much easier.

52. We use OCLC almost exclusively, except e-Book records, which come from vendors.

5. Outsourcing

Table 5.1: What functions or value-added services, if any, does your agency outsource to any degree? Authority control: obtaining new and updated authority records

	Yes	No
Entire Sample	45.71%	54.29%

Table 5.2: What functions or value-added services, if any, does your agency outsource to any degree? Authority control: obtaining new and updated authority records? Broken Out by FTE Student Enrollment

Student Enrollment	Yes	No
Less than 2,000	50.00%	50.00%
2,000 to 5,000	44.44%	55.56%
5,000 to 10,000	43.75%	56.25%
Over 10,000	45.45%	54.55%

Table 5.3: What functions or value-added services, if any, does your agency outsource to any degree? Authority control: obtaining new and updated authority records? Broken Out by Type of College

Type of College	Yes	No
Community College	10.00%	90.00%
4-Year Degree Granting College	41.38%	58.62%
MA or PHD Level Carnegie Class Institution	50.00%	50.00%
Level 1 or Level 2 Carnegie Class Research University	73.33%	26.67%

Table 5.4: What functions or value-added services, if any, does your agency outsource to any degree? Authority control: obtaining new and updated authority records? Broken Out by Public or Private Status

Public or Private Status	Yes	No
Public	30.95%	69.05%
Private	67.86%	32.14%

Table 5.5: What functions or value-added services, if any, does your agency outsource to any degree? Authority control: updating headings in bibliographic records

	Yes	No
Entire Sample	37.14%	62.86%

Table 5.6:   What functions or value-added services, if any, does your agency outsource to any degree? Authority control: updating headings in bibliographic records? Broken Out by FTE Student Enrollment

Student Enrollment	Yes	No
Less than 2,000	42.86%	57.14%
2,000 to 5,000	38.89%	61.11%
5,000 to 10,000	31.25%	68.75%
Over 10,000	36.36%	63.64%

Table 5.7:   What functions or value-added services, if any, does your agency outsource to any degree? Authority control: updating headings in bibliographic records? Broken Out by Type of College

Type of College	Yes	No
Community College	10.00%	90.00%
4-Year Degree Granting College	34.48%	65.52%
MA or PHD Level Carnegie Class Institution	43.75%	56.25%
Level 1 or Level 2 Carnegie Class Research University	53.33%	46.67%

Table 5.8:   What functions or value-added services, if any, does your agency outsource to any degree? Authority control: updating headings in bibliographic records? Broken Out by Public or Private Status

Public or Private Status	Yes	No
Public	23.81%	76.19%
Private	57.14%	42.86%

Table 5.9:   What functions or value-added services, if any, does your agency outsource to any degree? Bibliographic records: obtaining new bibliographic records

	Yes	No
Entire Sample	48.57%	51.43%

Table 5.10:   What functions or value-added services, if any, does your agency outsource to any degree? obtaining new bibliographic records? Broken Out by FTE Student Enrollment

Student Enrollment	Yes	No
Less than 2,000	42.86%	57.14%
2,000 to 5,000	27.78%	72.22%
5,000 to 10,000	50.00%	50.00%
Over 10,000	68.18%	31.82%

Table 5.11: **What functions or value-added services, if any, does your agency outsource to any degree? obtaining new bibliographic records? Broken Out by Type of College**

Type of College	Yes	No
Community College	20.00%	80.00%
4-Year Degree Granting College	48.28%	51.72%
MA or PHD Level Carnegie Class Institution	43.75%	56.25%
Level 1 or Level 2 Carnegie Class Research University	73.33%	26.67%

Table 5.12: **What functions or value-added services, if any, does your agency outsource to any degree? obtaining new bibliographic records? Broken Out by Public or Private Status**

Public or Private Status	Yes	No
Public	50.00%	50.00%
Private	46.43%	53.57%

Table 5.13: **What functions or value-added services, if any, does your agency outsource to any degree? Item records and inventory**

	Yes	No
Entire Sample	1.43%	98.57%

Table 5.14: **What functions or value-added services, if any, does your agency outsource to any degree? Item records and inventory? Broken Out by FTE Student Enrollment**

Student Enrollment	Yes	No
Less than 2,000	0.00%	100.00%
2,000 to 5,000	0.00%	100.00%
5,000 to 10,000	0.00%	100.00%
Over 10,000	4.55%	95.45%

Table 5.15: **What functions or value-added services, if any, does your agency outsource to any degree? Item records and inventory? Broken Out by Type of College**

Type of College	Yes	No
Community College	0.00%	100.00%
4-Year Degree Granting College	0.00%	100.00%
MA or PHD Level Carnegie Class Institution	6.25%	93.75%
Level 1 or Level 2 Carnegie Class Research University	0.00%	100.00%

Table 5.16: What functions or value-added services, if any, does your agency outsource to any degree? Item records and inventory? Broken Out by Public or Private Status

Public or Private Status	Yes	No
Public	0.00%	100.00%
Private	3.57%	96.43%

Table 5.17: What functions or value-added services, if any, does your agency outsource to any degree? Physical processing and bar-coding

Type of College	Yes	No
Entire Sample	22.86%	77.14%

Table 5.18: What functions or value-added services, if any, does your agency outsource to any degree? Physical processing and bar-coding? Broken Out by FTE Student Enrollment

Student Enrollment	Yes	No
Less than 2,000	21.43%	78.57%
2,000 to 5,000	5.56%	94.44%
5,000 to 10,000	18.75%	81.25%
Over 10,000	40.91%	59.09%

Table 5.19: What functions or value-added services, if any, does your agency outsource to any degree? Physical processing and bar-coding? Broken Out by Type of College

Type of College	Yes	No
Community College	10.00%	90.00%
4-Year Degree Granting College	13.79%	86.21%
MA or PHD Level Carnegie Class Institution	25.00%	75.00%
Level 1 or Level 2 Carnegie Class Research University	46.67%	53.33%

Table 5.20: What functions or value-added services, if any, does your agency outsource to any degree? Physical processing and bar-coding? Broken Out by Public or Private Status

Public or Private Status	Yes	No
Public	23.81%	76.19%
Private	21.43%	78.57%

Table 5.21: What functions or value-added services, if any, does your agency outsource to any degree? Table of contents notes added

	Yes	No
Entire Sample	21.43%	78.57%

Table 5.22: What functions or value-added services, if any, does your agency outsource to any degree? Table of contents notes added? Broken Out by FTE Student Enrollment

Student Enrollment	Yes	No
Less than 2,000	14.29%	85.71%
2,000 to 5,000	0.00%	100.00%
5,000 to 10,000	18.75%	81.25%
Over 10,000	45.45%	54.55%

Table 5.23: What functions or value-added services, if any, does your agency outsource to any degree? Table of contents notes added? Broken Out by Type of College

Type of College	Yes	No
Community College	10.00%	90.00%
4-Year Degree Granting College	6.90%	93.10%
MA or PHD Level Carnegie Class Institution	37.50%	62.50%
Level 1 or Level 2 Carnegie Class Research University	40.00%	60.00%

Table 5.24: What functions or value-added services, if any, does your agency outsource to any degree? Table of contents notes added? Broken Out by Public or Private Status

Public or Private Status	Yes	No
Public	28.57%	71.43%
Private	10.71%	89.29%

Table 5.25: What functions or value-added services, if any, does your agency outsource to any degree? Book reviews added

	Yes	No
Entire Sample	11.43%	88.57%

Table 5.26: What functions or value-added services, if any, does your agency outsource to any degree? Book reviews added? Broken Out by FTE Student Enrollment

Student Enrollment	Yes	No
Less than 2,000	14.29%	85.71%
2,000 to 5,000	5.56%	94.44%
5,000 to 10,000	6.25%	93.75%
Over 10,000	18.18%	81.82%

Table 5.27: What functions or value-added services, if any, does your agency outsource to any degree? Book reviews added? Broken Out by Type of College

Type of College	Yes	No
Community College	10.00%	90.00%
4-Year Degree Granting College	13.79%	86.21%
MA or PHD Level Carnegie Class Institution	12.50%	87.50%
Level 1 or Level 2 Carnegie Class Research University	6.67%	93.33%

Table 5.28: What functions or value-added services, if any, does your agency outsource to any degree? Book reviews added? Broken Out by Public or Private Status

Public or Private Status	Yes	No
Public	16.67%	83.33%
Private	3.57%	96.43%

Table 5.29: What functions or value-added services, if any, does your agency outsource to any degree? Book jackets added

	Yes	No
Entire Sample	25.71%	74.29%

Table 5.30: What functions or value-added services, if any, does your agency outsource to any degree? Book jackets added? Broken Out by FTE Student Enrollment

Student Enrollment	Yes	No
Less than 2,000	28.57%	71.43%
2,000 to 5,000	22.22%	77.78%
5,000 to 10,000	12.50%	87.50%
Over 10,000	36.36%	63.64%

Table 5.31: What functions or value-added services, if any, does your agency outsource to any degree? Book jackets added? Broken Out by Type of College

Type of College	Yes	No
Community College	0.00%	100.00%
4-Year Degree Granting College	27.59%	72.41%
MA or PHD Level Carnegie Class Institution	25.00%	75.00%
Level 1 or Level 2 Carnegie Class Research University	40.00%	60.00%

Table 5.32: What functions or value-added services, if any, does your agency outsource to any degree? Book jackets added? Broken Out by Public or Private Status

Public or Private Status	Yes	No
Public	19.05%	80.95%
Private	35.71%	64.29%

Table 5.33: What types of library resources are outsourced? Continuing resources (print)

	Yes	No
Entire Sample	4.29%	95.71%

Table 5.34: What types of library resources are outsourced? Continuing resources (print)? Broken Out by FTE Student Enrollment

Student Enrollment	Yes	No
Less than 2,000	0.00%	100.00%
2,000 to 5,000	0.00%	100.00%
5,000 to 10,000	0.00%	100.00%
Over 10,000	13.64%	86.36%

Table 5.35: What types of library resources are outsourced? Continuing resources (print)? Broken Out by Type of College

Type of College	Yes	No
Community College	10.00%	90.00%
4-Year Degree Granting College	3.45%	96.55%
MA or PHD Level Carnegie Class Institution	0.00%	100.00%
Level 1 or Level 2 Carnegie Class Research University	6.67%	93.33%

Table 5.36: What types of library resources are outsourced? Continuing resources (print)? Broken Out by Public or Private Status

Public or Private Status	Yes	No
Public	7.14%	92.86%
Private	0.00%	100.00%

Table 5.37: What types of library resources are outsourced? E-journals

	Yes	No
Entire Sample	35.71%	64.29%

Table 5.38: What types of library resources are outsourced? E-journals? Broken Out by FTE Student Enrollment

Student Enrollment	Yes	No
Less than 2,000	14.29%	85.71%
2,000 to 5,000	27.78%	72.22%
5,000 to 10,000	43.75%	56.25%
Over 10,000	50.00%	50.00%

Table 5.39: What types of library resources are outsourced? E-journals? Broken Out by Type of College

Type of College	Yes	No
Community College	10.00%	90.00%
4-Year Degree Granting College	27.59%	72.41%
MA or PHD Level Carnegie Class Institution	37.50%	62.50%
Level 1 or Level 2 Carnegie Class Research University	66.67%	33.33%

Table 5.40: What types of library resources are outsourced? E-journals? Broken Out by Public or Private Status

Public or Private Status	Yes	No
Public	38.10%	61.90%
Private	32.14%	67.86%

Table 5.41: What types of library resources are outsourced? E-books

	Yes	No
Entire Sample	44.29%	55.71%

Table 5.42:   What types of library resources are outsourced? E-books? Broken Out by FTE Student Enrollment

Student Enrollment	Yes	No
Less than 2,000	57.14%	42.86%
2,000 to 5,000	27.78%	72.22%
5,000 to 10,000	43.75%	56.25%
Over 10,000	50.00%	50.00%

Table 5.43:   What types of library resources are outsourced? E-books? Broken Out by Type of College

Type of College	Yes	No
Community College	30.00%	70.00%
4-Year Degree Granting College	37.93%	62.07%
MA or PHD Level Carnegie Class Institution	43.75%	56.25%
Level 1 or Level 2 Carnegie Class Research University	66.67%	33.33%

Table 5.44:   What types of library resources are outsourced? E-books? Broken Out by Public or Private Status

Public or Private Status	Yes	No
Public	42.86%	57.14%
Private	46.43%	53.57%

Table 5.45:   What types of library resources are outsourced? AV Formats

	Yes	No
Entire Sample	4.29%	95.71%

Table 5.46:   What types of library resources are outsourced? AV Formats? Broken Out by FTE Student Enrollment

Student Enrollment	Yes	No
Less than 2,000	0.00%	100.00%
2,000 to 5,000	5.56%	94.44%
5,000 to 10,000	6.25%	93.75%
Over 10,000	4.55%	95.45%

Table 5.47:   What types of library resources are outsourced? AV Formats? Broken Out by Type of College

Type of College	Yes	No
Community College	0.00%	100.00%
4-Year Degree Granting College	6.90%	93.10%
MA or PHD Level Carnegie Class Institution	0.00%	100.00%
Level 1 or Level 2 Carnegie Class Research University	6.67%	93.33%

Table 5.48:   What types of library resources are outsourced? AV Formats? Broken Out by Public or Private Status

Public or Private Status	Yes	No
Public	2.38%	97.62%
Private	7.14%	92.86%

Table 5.49:   What types of library resources are outsourced? Foreign language resources for which the cataloging agency has no expertise

	Yes	No
Entire Sample	8.57%	91.43%

Table 5.50:   What types of library resources are outsourced? Foreign language resources for which the cataloging agency has no expertise? Broken Out by FTE Student Enrollment

Student Enrollment	Yes	No
Less than 2,000	7.14%	92.86%
2,000 to 5,000	5.56%	94.44%
5,000 to 10,000	18.75%	81.25%
Over 10,000	4.55%	95.45%

Table 5.51:   What types of library resources are outsourced? Foreign language resources for which the cataloging agency has no expertise? Broken Out by Type of College

Type of College	Yes	No
Community College	0.00%	100.00%
4-Year Degree Granting College	6.90%	93.10%
MA or PHD Level Carnegie Class Institution	12.50%	87.50%
Level 1 or Level 2 Carnegie Class Research University	13.33%	86.67%

Table 5.52:   What types of library resources are outsourced? Foreign language resources for which the cataloging agency has no expertise? Broken Out by Public or Private Status

Public or Private Status	Yes	No
Public	7.14%	92.86%
Private	10.71%	89.29%

Table 5.53:   What types of library resources are outsourced? Other Digital Formats

	Yes	No
Entire Sample	5.71%	94.29%

Table 5.54:   What types of library resources are outsourced? Other Digital Formats? Broken Out by FTE Student Enrollment

Student Enrollment	Yes	No
Less than 2,000	0.00%	100.00%
2,000 to 5,000	5.56%	94.44%
5,000 to 10,000	0.00%	100.00%
Over 10,000	13.64%	86.36%

Table 5.55:   What types of library resources are outsourced? Other Digital Formats? Broken Out by Type of College

Type of College	Yes	No
Community College	10.00%	90.00%
4-Year Degree Granting College	3.45%	96.55%
MA or PHD Level Carnegie Class Institution	6.25%	93.75%
Level 1 or Level 2 Carnegie Class Research University	6.67%	93.33%

Table 5.56:   What types of library resources are outsourced? Other Digital Formats? Broken Out by Public or Private Status

Public or Private Status	Yes	No
Public	9.52%	90.48%
Private	0.00%	100.00%

Table 5.57:   What types of library resources are outsourced? Materials in Cataloging Backlogs

	Yes	No
Entire Sample	2.86%	97.14%

Table 5.58: **What types of library resources are outsourced? Materials in Cataloging Backlogs? Broken Out by FTE Student Enrollment**

Student Enrollment	Yes	No
Less than 2,000	7.14%	92.86%
2,000 to 5,000	0.00%	100.00%
5,000 to 10,000	6.25%	93.75%
Over 10,000	0.00%	100.00%

Table 5.59: **What types of library resources are outsourced? Materials in Cataloging Backlogs? Broken Out by Type of College**

Type of College	Yes	No
Community College	0.00%	100.00%
4-Year Degree Granting College	3.45%	96.55%
MA or PHD Level Carnegie Class Institution	0.00%	100.00%
Level 1 or Level 2 Carnegie Class Research University	6.67%	93.33%

Table 5.60: **What types of library resources are outsourced? Materials in Cataloging Backlogs? Broken Out by Public or Private Status**

Public or Private Status	Yes	No
Public	2.38%	97.62%
Private	3.57%	96.43%

Table 5.61: **What types of library resources are outsourced? All Materials are outsourced**

	Yes	No
Entire Sample	0.00%	100.00%

If you have outsourced library resources, please briefly explain why you outsourced certain types of library resources.

1. Large batches that are available for quick download.
2. Most books arrive shelf-ready as it is cheaper and faster than doing them in-house. E-gov. docs are outsourced as no one has time to catalog them. Some music scores are outsourced as we have little expertise in cataloging scores.
3. The only things we outsource are our print monographs, which we get shelf-ready and our e-journals for which we receive SerialsSolutions records. Print monographs are simple enough that we could be assured of reasonable quality in cataloging and it sped up time to get materials to shelf. Keeping e-journal records up to date is complicated it made sense to take advantage of the services of SerialsSolutions.
4. We subscribe to various electronic sets. We have no non-Roman language expertise on staff.
5. We had a small foreign language backlog that we outsourced. We also created brief records for full-text e-journals we have access to via databases from our link resolver information, which could be construed as outsourcing. We also get records for a couple of substantial e-book collections.
6. Time. We only have 2 cataloguing staff and half a dozen acquisitions staff so to physically process and/or catalogue everything would be too much time.
7. To improve time-to-shelf and lack of sufficient local staffing (this is not a bad thing, I believe in outsourcing, but just a fact that we don't have enough staff to do these things locally)
8. Part of consortium effort.
9. Lack of expertise in non-Latin languages, lack of format/subject expertise, ability to get the newest materials to the shelves faster.
10. We obtained Marcive's Documents without Shelves for Government Documents. Other than some duplication of titles, these have been easy to load and a great resource for our patrons.
11. Outsourcing is more cost effective and time saving.
12. Small temporary backlog, Lack of funds to hire student workers.
13. We were given a large gift of books with a donation to contract a cataloger to catalog them.
14. We use vendor provided catalog records for e-books and e-journals because we do not have the staff time to catalog these materials ourselves and believe that these materials are a useful service to provide our patrons.
15. Can't keep up with authority control, use SFX to help provide access to increasing number of e-journals
16. Binding and basic processing. No in-house bindery, processing is cost-effective.
17. We do bulk loads of e-book packages. Our consortium supplies e-journals, and we buy extra subscriptions.
18. We purchase records from Serials Solutions for e-journals and e-books because it would be too impossible to keep track of holdings changes for all the serials & books in all our databases. We purchase records for large collections of e-books and other e-resources (such as streaming media) because the sheer number of items makes it impossible to catalog them a timely manner. We recently outsourced the cataloging of our Cyrillic purchases because the person who cataloged Russian went on extended medical leave and there was no one else with that language expertise.
19. We are also outsourcing print books. We keep losing staff as they retire or get different jobs. We are also looking to move existing staff to working on the "hidden" collections, digital library materials, ETDs, IR materials, etc.
20. We get bibliographic records for firm-ordered books from our main vendor. This was done when our department lost one of its long-time catalogers to retirement. While we could take the long view in terms of getting all purchased materials cataloged and processed within a fiscal year, we did not want materials to sit on the shelves for more than a month.
21. Bibliographic records: AV (added to library responsibilities with no increase in staff; about 1/2 still cataloged in-house); US government documents (we're a depository), e-book collections; e-journals; non-Roman alphabets Chinese/Japanese/Korean/Arabic titles (we can do cyrillic). Authority records: new records for GovDocs & other large files of outsourced bibs (not AV); updates to all our authority records Authority processing: automatic authority control processing in our III system flips bib headings to match incoming authorized headings; still requires a lot of cleanup and checking.
22. E-books, e-audio and e-video that come to us in large numbers have to be outsourced because we don't have the staff to catalog them individually. We use PromptCat for book cataloging, as our Acquisitions department uses YBP and we coordinate full record download for YBP orders with them. We outsource

authority control for DLC books, modifying cataloging record headings, because they are the largest number of materials received and the hit rate for authority matches is the highest, giving us more for the money we spend.

23. N/A

24. N/A

25. For e-books, ease of access to large collections; for book jackets and reviews, convenience for the patron.

26. The availability and quality of records met our needs/standards. The number of e-resources we collect is beyond our ability to locally catalog so vendor records are relied upon, when appropriate.

27. We also outsource our gov doc records since the load was too much for current staff.

28. Turkish and Hebrew language materials, some Russian.

29. We get MARC records from vendors when subscribing to large databases such as Early American Imprints as well as records to those full-text journals available from JSTOR and EBSCO databases.

30. We outsourced print monographs because of budget. We outsourced e-books and e-journals (in terms of accepting vendor records) because the high number of these resources does not allow for effective one by one processing.

31. OCLC less expensive.

32. Cost/time savings; particularly for large sets of e-book records licensed.

33. We outsourced cataloging of most new material. This resulted in positions being eliminated so I assume there was a positive financial result.

34. Print books, don't have time or staff to copy catalog all that come in; need to concentrate on foreign language materials, unique formats and digital collections.

35. To free up personnel for other departments

36. Use vendor supplied records because of volume.

37. N/A

38. We outsource the vast majority of electronic resource acquisition, cataloging, management, etc. to the Carnegie Research 1 University system of which we are part, paying a per FTE fee for access. We manage any e-journals, e-books or other digital resources we obtain outside the shared system, and we have an autonomous Dspace repository. We also outsource some physical processing of print (i.e. shelf ready), and obtain our bib records through YBP.

39. Time. E-Books come in packages with 26,000 records at a time. There is no way we could accommodate that into our workflow.

40. This is really just as far as I know. We have access to the major databases, but that's a bout all, I think.

41. OhioLINK and our sub-consortium, OPAL, provide records for some of the online materials to which we have access through them. OPAL purchases authority control through LTI, and federal document records through MARCIVE.

42. We use shelf-ready services and we buy records for large batches of electronic materials, both e-books and e-journals. Large e-packages are too difficult to keep up with manually. Shelf ready is a logical choice as it frees up our highly experienced catalogers to concentrate on more challenging materials.

43. We have acquired cataloging records for large sets of e-resources (e.g., 125,000 records for the Congressional Serial Set). We send current cataloging records to MARCIVE for authority work. We receive our entire US depository cataloging from MARCIVE.

44. N/A

45. When system was first brought in early 1990's, we had Blackwell do authority. Not happy with results, so won't do again, but gave us a starting point.

46. We purchase collections from Ebrary and NetLibrary -- Is this what do you mean? We use their MARC records.

What are the criteria you use, if any, to analyze and determine the best sources of high quality records for outsourced materials?

1. Just get them from the vendor where we purchase the item. No criteria.
2. Cost.
3. We have requested only PCC or LC records for our shelf-ready books. If there is not a PCC or LC record, we catalog in house.
4. We find OCLC records thoroughly adequate. Electronic record sets are mildly scrutinized for quality.
5. Primarily, we get records from the vendors we're acquiring.
6. Not sure - the subject staff have been briefed but not fully trained on what to look for.
7. Basic adherence to accepted descriptive practices, LCSH, cost
8. Language ability available from a vendor, price, records which meet minimum standards of fullness (e.g., with subjects, call numbers, etc.), value-added services, customer service.
9. Spot checking. I've used these before and so trust the quality of Marcive's records.
10. EncLev =1 or blank.
11. LC Records.
12. Take a sample look at what is provided and determine if it's god quality.
13. We request sample records and study them for completeness, accuracy, and the amount of editing required to bring them up to our standards.
14. N/A
15. The librarian catalogers analyze sample records before they are bulk loaded and suggest any needed changes. Our consortium's IT office helps with these loads, including doing any MarcEdit work.
16. Mostly, we take what vendors offer, but we review each record load before it goes in the catalog and make appropriate changes as needed using MARCEdit. In the case of the Cyrillic records, we reviewed sample records several times before signing up for the service, and suggested changes in the records to be delivered so that the records would conform to national cataloging standards.
17. None. We are using OCLC WCP (Promptcat) in coordination with our approval and main firm order vendor.
18. Since most of our outsourced bibs are for packaged purchases, we take what we can get and do cleanup after as time permits.
19. For e-resources: correct MARC format and record quality, full record with LC class and LCSH preferred, accurate description, authority control applied, URL to the direct title, permanent resource usually purchased or with a renewing subscription.
20. N/A
21. N/A
22. Not sure; decisions made by the Library director.
23. Access points, cost.
24. Source of cataloging, level of customization available.
25. Priority 1: adherence to standards. Priority 2: completeness of information. Priority 3: costs/record.
26. I don't see the records that come back.
27. Our outsourcing vendor for monographs provides us with DLC records when available. We accept vendor records for e-books and Serials Solutions records for e-journals. Some vendor records are better than others.
28. Cataloger review.
29. Free is best. We accept any record and make global changes to upgrade when possible.
30. N/A
31. Are there subject headings? Is the bibliographic information such as author correct? Is the MARC coding correct?
32. Review of records prior to loading in ILS.
33. N/A
34. There is only one source for our records, but they are high quality: LC classification, subject headings, accuracy.
35. All of those decisions are made at a higher level than our institution.
36. LC/PCC records are preferred, but not required.
36. We participate with the catalogers at our main library to create RFP's for vendors to bid on based on quality, quantity, reliability, and experience.

37. IF I were to outsource: Are there any misspellings? Are the subject headings adequate and appropriate? Is the call number correct? Are there contents notes and summary statements? Is the item processed neatly?
38. Necessity . . .

Table 5.62:   What quality control methods do you use, if any, to assure vendor supplied records are accurate and complete: Use MarcEdit or other MARC editor to preview records and globally edit to local standards prior to loading?

	Yes	No
Entire Sample	42.86%	57.14%

Table 5.63:   What quality control methods do you use, if any, to assure vendor supplied records are accurate and complete: Use MarcEdit or other MARC editor to preview records and globally edit to local standards prior to loading? Broken Out by FTE Student Enrollment

Student Enrollment	Yes	No
Less than 2,000	35.71%	64.29%
2,000 to 5,000	38.89%	61.11%
5,000 to 10,000	56.25%	43.75%
Over 10,000	40.91%	59.09%

Table 5.64:   What quality control methods do you use, if any, to assure vendor supplied records are accurate and complete: Use MarcEdit or other MARC editor to preview records and globally edit to local standards prior to loading? Broken Out by Type of College

Type of College	Yes	No
Community College	0.00%	100.00%
4-Year Degree Granting College	48.28%	51.72%
MA or PHD Level Carnegie Class Institution	43.75%	56.25%
Level 1 or Level 2 Carnegie Class Research University	60.00%	40.00%

Table 5.65:   What quality control methods do you use, if any, to assure vendor supplied records are accurate and complete: Use MarcEdit or other MARC editor to preview records and globally edit to local standards prior to loading? Broken Out by Public or Private Status

Public or Private Status	Yes	No
Public	33.33%	66.67%
Private	57.14%	42.86%

Table 5.66: **What quality control methods do you use, if any, to assure vendor supplied records are accurate and complete: Use local integrated system to review loaded records and globally edit to local standards, whenever possible?**

	Yes	No
Entire Sample	31.43%	68.57%

Table 5.67: **What quality control methods do you use, if any, to assure vendor supplied records are accurate and complete: Use local integrated system to review loaded records and globally edit to local standards, whenever possible? Broken Out by FTE Student Enrollment**

Student Enrollment	Yes	No
Less than 2,000	35.71%	64.29%
2,000 to 5,000	33.33%	66.67%
5,000 to 10,000	37.50%	62.50%
Over 10,000	22.73%	77.27%

Table 5.68: **What quality control methods do you use, if any, to assure vendor supplied records are accurate and complete: Use local integrated system to review loaded records and globally edit to local standards, whenever possible? Broken Out by Type of College**

Type of College	Yes	No
Community College	10.00%	90.00%
4-Year Degree Granting College	31.03%	68.97%
MA or PHD Level Carnegie Class Institution	43.75%	56.25%
Level 1 or Level 2 Carnegie Class Research University	33.33%	66.67%

Table 5.69: **What quality control methods do you use, if any, to assure vendor supplied records are accurate and complete: Use local integrated system to review loaded records and globally edit to local standards, whenever possible? Broken Out by Public or Private Status**

Public or Private Status	Yes	No
Public	30.95%	69.05%
Private	32.14%	67.86%

Table 5.70: **What quality control methods do you use, if any, to assure vendor supplied records are accurate and complete: Spot check vendor records, whenever complete review isn't possible?**

	Yes	No
Entire Sample	38.57%	61.43%

Table 5.71: What quality control methods do you use, if any, to assure vendor supplied records are accurate and complete: Spot check vendor records, whenever complete review isn't possible? Broken Out by FTE Student Enrollment

Student Enrollment	Yes	No
Less than 2,000	50.00%	50.00%
2,000 to 5,000	38.89%	61.11%
5,000 to 10,000	31.25%	68.75%
Over 10,000	36.36%	63.64%

Table 5.72: What quality control methods do you use, if any, to assure vendor supplied records are accurate and complete: Spot check vendor records, whenever complete review isn't possible? Broken Out by Type of College

Type of College	Yes	No
Community College	10.00%	90.00%
4-Year Degree Granting College	41.38%	58.62%
MA or PHD Level Carnegie Class Institution	43.75%	56.25%
Level 1 or Level 2 Carnegie Class Research University	46.67%	53.33%

Table 5.73: What quality control methods do you use, if any, to assure vendor supplied records are accurate and complete: Spot check vendor records, whenever complete review isn't possible? Broken Out by Public or Private Status

Public or Private Status	Yes	No
Public	30.95%	69.05%
Private	50.00%	50.00%

Table 5.74: What quality control methods do you use, if any, to assure vendor supplied records are accurate and complete: Always spot check all vendor records?

	Yes	No
Entire Sample	21.43%	78.57%

Table 5.75: What quality control methods do you use, if any, to assure vendor supplied records are accurate and complete: Always spot check all vendor records? Broken Out by FTE Student Enrollment

Student Enrollment	Yes	No
Less than 2,000	14.29%	85.71%
2,000 to 5,000	27.78%	72.22%
5,000 to 10,000	37.50%	62.50%
Over 10,000	9.09%	90.91%

Table 5.76:   What quality control methods do you use, if any, to assure vendor supplied records are accurate and complete: Always spot check all vendor records? Broken Out by Type of College

Type of College	Yes	No
Community College	40.00%	60.00%
4-Year Degree Granting College	27.59%	72.41%
MA or PHD Level Carnegie Class Institution	12.50%	87.50%
Level 1 or Level 2 Carnegie Class Research University	6.67%	93.33%

Table 5.77:   What quality control methods do you use, if any, to assure vendor supplied records are accurate and complete: Always spot check all vendor records? Broken Out by Public or Private Status

Public or Private Status	Yes	No
Public	19.05%	80.95%
Private	25.00%	75.00%

Table 5.78:   What quality control methods do you use, if any, to assure vendor supplied records are accurate and complete: No or minimal review performed?

	Yes	No
Entire Sample	15.71%	84.29%

Table 5.79:   What quality control methods do you use, if any, to assure vendor supplied records are accurate and complete: No or minimal review performed? Broken Out by FTE Student Enrollment

Student Enrollment	Yes	No
Less than 2,000	7.14%	92.86%
2,000 to 5,000	16.67%	83.33%
5,000 to 10,000	6.25%	93.75%
Over 10,000	27.27%	72.73%

Table 5.80: **What quality control methods do you use, if any, to assure vendor supplied records are accurate and complete: No or minimal review performed? Broken Out by Type of College**

Type of College	Yes	No
Community College	30.00%	70.00%
4-Year Degree Granting College	3.45%	96.55%
MA or PHD Level Carnegie Class Institution	25.00%	75.00%
Level 1 or Level 2 Carnegie Class Research University	20.00%	80.00%

Table 5.81: **What quality control methods do you use, if any, to assure vendor supplied records are accurate and complete: No or minimal review performed? Broken Out by Public or Private Status**

Public or Private Status	Yes	No
Public	21.43%	78.57%
Private	7.14%	92.86%

What quality control methods do you use, if any, to assure vendor supplied records are accurate and complete: Other (please specify)

1. Check import report and request books with minimal records to be passed to cataloguing.
2. No vendor records other than consortium engagement of vendor loading of authority file.
3. Hope patrons who notice problems let us know (applies to entire catalog).
4. We review the records using our quality standards for e-resources.
5. The local system (III) generates reports if potential errors are present.

6. State of Cataloging Education in Library Schools

What are your opinions and thoughts regarding cataloging education in present and future ALA-accredited library and information schools?

1. There is not enough time to practice it.
2. It no longer seems to be important. Many new librarians have minimal classes.
3. Cataloging needs to be a requirement.
4. More emphasis needs to be made on teaching cataloging practices and on the best practices for metadata creation.
5. Very little experience. Assistants have arrived well-trained by MLS programs.
6. It's hard to cover everything you need to know in a 3 hour course, but the decrease in required cataloging somewhat disturbs me.
7. N/A - I am in the UK. I feel that unfortunately in the UK it is being squeezed out a bit.
8. Students are taught how to originally catalog, as if that is what most of us are doing. While pedagogically, that probably makes sense, students need to learn how to originally catalog in order to understand the principles of information organization and in order to assess quality, they also need to understand that most of what they will be doing is supervising support staff, identifying & managing record outsourcing, record transformation and loading, assessing cost & value, negotiating relationships with vendors & IT staff.
9. Library schools don't teach cataloging anymore, so "cataloging education" is something of an oxymoron. What LIS do offer is all theoretical, at a much higher level than new graduates will need, which means all the practical education and training is left to the employer after hire.
10. Need to graduate people who are knowledgeable about metadata and access issues.
11. Courses via the OCLC Training Portal, webinar, hands on workshops with other professionals are helpful for networking face to face.
12. I don't think that there are enough cataloging courses offered. I took 4 of these courses, all that were offered, but would have appreciated more.
13. Having just graduated from library school, I had very minimal training even though I took most of the cataloging courses (more the teacher than university fault - she has since been replaced); learned most of what I know from working as a copy cataloger on campus in the music department. Unsure of how cataloging education is nationwide.
14. Poor. There is no interest in cataloging. It's an elective, which no one elects.
15. Cataloguing classes should be a requirement for students.
16. As far as I can see, there is a lack of cataloging education.
17. We have given preference to those who had some type of library experience, such as volunteer work or an internship. In my experience many library schools do not provide the detailed hands-on type of cataloging education required to do the job.
18. Cataloging and Metadata studies should continue to be taught at ALA accredited colleges.
19. This doesn't really apply to us. We have not hired a professionally trained cataloger since 1990 (me). All other departmental hires have been paraprofessionals with no ALA-accredited cataloging education. I hope to hire people who have had previous library or tech services training if possible.
20. Organization of Knowledge theory must be taught. Bib record frameworks change, but indexing and controlled vocabularies (thesauri) are vital, especially in concert with keyword approaches.
21. I feel that cataloging education needs to strengthen its ALA accredited library and information. All librarians need some exposure to cataloging. Public service librarians can do copy cataloging.
22. The first cataloging course should be required in order to earn an ALA-accredited MLS. The second course should be strongly encouraged for most students. I earned my MLS before the Internet even existed, but I hope today they offer classes beyond those two, covering metadata schemes in depth.
23. On the one hand, I find it increasingly difficult to talk with newly hired librarians who are not catalogers because their library school education has usually covered very little (if anything) about cataloging, the MARC record, or bibliographic description. So we lack a common language with which to discuss perceived problems of display or functioning in the online catalog. But on the other hand, I don't see how a library school could adequately prepare someone to be a professional cataloger. There is just too

much to learn, and too much that has to be learned in the context of practice. Cataloging is a science in that there are "rules", but it is also an art. The all-important "catalogers judgment" cannot be developed in a classroom.

24. More of it is needed. Cataloging is a good foundation for any library position in the library.

25. Librarians not intending on going into cataloging are being poorly served by not being trained on how catalog records and discovery systems work (comment on question #27-not recent hires).

26. Not high. Difficult to teach cataloging without a catalog to work with. Traditional cataloging focuses on individual record creation rather than the relationships between works (through author, subject, FRBR work/expression/manifestation, classification that are a big part of what cataloging should be. Other metadata & technical aspects (indexing, database structure) take up more time. Many folks coming out of library school haven't taken cataloging; I wonder if they know enough to really help our patrons.

27. Cataloging and metadata again need to be a core component of a library education. Cataloging professors should be hired, and cataloging theory and practical courses should be taught by tenured or fulltime faculty in the field, not assigned to a non-cataloging professor. Into to the organization of materials courses are not enough.

28. I am the only professional cataloger in my library, and I graduated over 30 years ago, so I don't really know. I can't answer the following question because we have not hired any recent graduates in cataloging.

29. There is a serious need for more practical and in-depth cataloging classes in library schools.

30. Based on what I see on AutoCat, it seems that Cataloging is not being given a high priority in LIS programs. With the new tools such as RDA, FRBR, etc. more emphasis needs to be placed in learning (1) theory and (2) practice.

31. ALA needs to put more emphasis on cataloging, but also more work on the future integration of library information with the wider world of information, i.e. the internet.

32. It is currently insufficient.

33. Should include experience with XML, Perl, regular expressions.

34. For awhile it has been in decline, which is a mistake, and needs to be re-emphasized.

35. The knowledge of basic cataloging is missing from many "newbie" library school graduates. The trend seems to be going towards metadata but even that knowledge seems minimal at best.

36. The day of the scholar-librarian is either gone or disappearing. In its place technical skills are required. This is not all bad, but needs to be put into perspective. Are highly skilled technicians equipped to put their collections into perspective in their own libraries and in comparison with others in the nation and in the world? We do live in the age of World-Cat after all. Katie Henderson, my catalog teacher at University of Illinois Champaign/Urbana, used to say that one is not cataloging the perfect record for the expert, but "simply to help people find the ****** book." The best that the cataloger can do is to try to imagine how a patron will look for a particular item and to make it easier to do so. In recent years I have taken more time to insert 505 contents notes and 520 summaries of contents into the records. The computer can then find keywords and help a patron find what he/she is looking for even if access to the shelves is denied or impossible. A fuller description of the item should be the goal - but that is also time-consuming. It's a tradeoff.

37. WE need to continue to provide cataloging courses in library school

38. I think that cataloging education is still being represented in library schools but I'm not sure that it is being taught as often or as well as it should be. Perhaps the conceptual split between "cataloging" and "metadata" needs to be done away with. It's ALL metadata. The reality of today's catalogers is that they need to be prepared to work on a variety of resources using a variety of standards. At the same time, the use of multiple standards is evolving as libraries get heavily invested in electronic resources and digital projects and information on those standards is more often learned on an ad hoc basis. What library schools might consider doing (and I think some of them have) is to contribute to the professional development of working catalogers who need to learn these standards by offering courses that are longer than a webinar and shorter than a typical semester long class.

39. Some schools have wonderful programs.

40. Very few places are teaching cataloging and very few qualified instructors exist, which will create a shortage of people who are well qualified out of school. Fewer places have resources to adequately train in-house, and are expecting entry-level catalogers to come in with experience. If students aren't getting instruction & experience (i.e. internships) in programs, I'm not sure how we're going to continue to have enough catalogers to fill positions.

41. Not sufficient

42. I believe cataloging education is in peril. Cataloging is being outsourced at an alarming rate. Library schools are more interested in information organization and manipulation than AACR2R rules.

43. Most schools have gone away from a basic cataloging to a generic introduction to technical services. Hence much training is done at point of hiring.

44. As an adjunct who teaches cataloging, there needs to be effort to link the theoretical to the practical so new librarians have an idea why a catalog acts the way it does and how the bib records affect it.

45. Cataloging is in such flux with standards RDA, FRBR and other metadata schemas that I am sure it is hard to teach all aspects of cataloging but organization of information, providing quality data, pushing out data to users and reusing data are the principles of cataloging that continue to be important. I think cataloging education could address examining workflow processes, using technological solutions in processes, and streamline processes would be a good exercise for students. Identifying the best practices.

46. Not impressive. However, RDA will likely be easier to teach than AACR2. MARC coding will likely be easier with more integrated help in ILSs.

47. You don't need an MLS to really be a good cataloger. Everybody has trained some little chippy right out of library school only to have them become somebody's boss, maybe even their own. Needless to say, these people end up being about as popular as a hooker at a Moral Majority meeting!

48. Since I graduated in 1984, and don't know anyone who graduated less than 20 years ago, I don't feel qualified to have an opinion. All the evidence I could base it on is vague, general complaints on the lists.

49. The specifics of metadata creation, MARC or other, will continue to be best learned on the job – library schools should concentrate on teaching principles of organization that can be applied to many metadata languages.

50. It's really hopping, isn't it?

51. Inadequate. Courses seem to deal more with the philosophy of cataloging without touching on the practical needs of the user. For question 27, I didn't answer because we haven't hired anyone recently.

52. One cataloguing course is not enough. At least 2 or 3 should be required. More hands-on cataloguing experience also needs to be provided.

53. I don't think actual cataloging is taught to a great degree. People who have come on staff or people who have done internship are totally blown away by cataloging. We figure it takes a copy cataloging person about 4-6 months to be up to standards.

54. Not enough of it... Should be required.

55. Basic cataloging instruction is valuable in seeing how records are put together and information is needed for the end-user.

56. There is none.

Table 6.1:   Please categorize the preparedness of your recent library hires in the following cataloging and metadata competencies, philosophies, principles and practices: Classification Systems?

	Not Prepared at All	Minimally Prepared	Prepared	Well Prepared
Entire Sample	10.00%	50.00%	24.00%	16.00%

Table 6.2:   Please categorize the preparedness of your recent library hires in the following cataloging and metadata competencies, philosophies, principles and practices: Classification Systems? Broken Out by FTE Student Enrollment

Student Enrollment	Not Prepared at All	Minimally Prepared	Prepared	Well Prepared
Less than 2,000	11.11%	55.56%	22.22%	11.11%
2,000 to 5,000	30.77%	30.77%	30.77%	7.69%
5,000 to 10,000	0.00%	46.15%	30.77%	23.08%
Over 10,000	0.00%	66.67%	13.33%	20.00%

Table 6.3:   Please categorize the preparedness of your recent library hires in the following cataloging and metadata competencies, philosophies, principles and practices: Classification Systems? Broken Out by Type of College

Type of College	Not Prepared at All	Minimally Prepared	Prepared	Well Prepared
Community College	0.00%	66.67%	16.67%	16.67%
4-Year Degree Granting College	14.29%	42.86%	28.57%	14.29%
MA or PHD Level Carnegie Class Institution	20.00%	50.00%	20.00%	10.00%
Level 1 or Level 2 Carnegie Class Research University	0.00%	53.85%	23.08%	23.08%

Table 6.4: Please categorize the preparedness of your recent library hires in the following cataloging and metadata competencies, philosophies, principles and practices: Classification Systems? Broken Out by Public or Private Status

Public or Private Status	Not Prepared at All	Minimally Prepared	Prepared	Well Prepared
Public	0.00%	58.06%	25.81%	16.13%
Private	26.32%	36.84%	21.05%	15.79%

Table 6.5: Please categorize the preparedness of your recent library hires in the following cataloging and metadata competencies, philosophies, principles and practices: Subject /Genre Thesauri Systems?

	Not Prepared at All	Minimally Prepared	Prepared	Well Prepared
Entire Sample	14.58%	54.17%	22.92%	8.33%

Table 6.6: Please categorize the preparedness of your recent library hires in the following cataloging and metadata competencies, philosophies, principles and practices: Subject /Genre Thesauri Systems? Broken Out by FTE Student Enrollment

Student Enrollment	Not Prepared at All	Minimally Prepared	Prepared	Well Prepared
Less than 2,000	0.00%	66.67%	11.11%	22.22%
2,000 to 5,000	41.67%	41.67%	8.33%	8.33%
5,000 to 10,000	7.69%	38.46%	46.15%	7.69%
Over 10,000	7.14%	71.43%	21.43%	0.00%

Table 6.7: Please categorize the preparedness of your recent library hires in the following cataloging and metadata competencies, philosophies, principles and practices: Subject /Genre Thesauri Systems? Broken Out by Type of College

Type of College	Not Prepared at All	Minimally Prepared	Prepared	Well Prepared
Community College	0.00%	83.33%	0.00%	16.67%
4-Year Degree Granting College	10.00%	60.00%	20.00%	10.00%
MA or PHD Level Carnegie Class Institution	44.44%	22.22%	33.33%	0.00%
Level 1 or Level 2 Carnegie Class Research University	7.69%	53.85%	30.77%	7.69%

Table 6.8: Please categorize the preparedness of your recent library hires in the following cataloging and metadata competencies, philosophies, principles and practices: Subject /Genre Thesauri Systems? Broken Out by Public or Private Status

Public or Private Status	Not Prepared at All	Minimally Prepared	Prepared	Well Prepared
Public	6.67%	63.33%	26.67%	3.33%
Private	27.78%	38.89%	16.67%	16.67%

Table 6.9: Please categorize the preparedness of your recent library hires in the following cataloging and metadata competencies, philosophies, principles and practices: Classification and Subject /Genre Analysis Principles, Rules and Tools?

	Not Prepared at All	Minimally Prepared	Prepared	Well Prepared
Entire Sample	21.28%	55.32%	14.89%	8.51%

Table 6.10: Please categorize the preparedness of your recent library hires in the following cataloging and metadata competencies, philosophies, principles and practices: Classification and Subject /Genre Analysis Principles, Rules and Tools? Broken Out by FTE Student Enrollment

Student Enrollment	Not Prepared at All	Minimally Prepared	Prepared	Well Prepared
Less than 2,000	11.11%	55.56%	22.22%	11.11%
2,000 to 5,000	66.67%	25.00%	0.00%	8.33%
5,000 to 10,000	0.00%	75.00%	16.67%	8.33%
Over 10,000	7.14%	64.29%	21.43%	7.14%

Table 6.11: Please categorize the preparedness of your recent library hires in the following cataloging and metadata competencies, philosophies, principles and practices: Classification and Subject /Genre Analysis Principles, Rules and Tools? Broken Out by Type of College

Type of College	Not Prepared at All	Minimally Prepared	Prepared	Well Prepared
Community College	0.00%	83.33%	0.00%	16.67%
4-Year Degree Granting College	30.00%	50.00%	15.00%	5.00%
MA or PHD Level Carnegie Class Institution	44.44%	33.33%	11.11%	11.11%
Level 1 or Level 2 Carnegie Class Research University	0.00%	66.67%	25.00%	8.33%

Table 6.12: Please categorize the preparedness of your recent library hires in the following cataloging and metadata competencies, philosophies, principles and practices: Classification and Subject /Genre Analysis Principles, Rules and Tools? Broken Out by Public or Private Status

Public or Private Status	Not Prepared at All	Minimally Prepared	Prepared	Well Prepared
Public	10.00%	66.67%	16.67%	6.67%
Private	41.18%	35.29%	11.76%	11.76%

Table 6.13: Please categorize the preparedness of your recent library hires in the following cataloging and metadata competencies, philosophies, principles and practices: Java and PERL Script Applications?

	Not Prepared at All	Minimally Prepared	Prepared	Well Prepared
Entire Sample	64.44%	22.22%	11.11%	2.22%

Table 6.14: Please categorize the preparedness of your recent library hires in the following cataloging and metadata competencies, philosophies, principles and practices: Java and PERL Script Applications? Broken Out by FTE Student Enrollment

Student Enrollment	Not Prepared at All	Minimally Prepared	Prepared	Well Prepared
Less than 2,000	62.50%	25.00%	12.50%	0.00%
2,000 to 5,000	66.67%	16.67%	16.67%	0.00%
5,000 to 10,000	54.55%	36.36%	9.09%	0.00%
Over 10,000	71.43%	14.29%	7.14%	7.14%

Table 6.15: Please categorize the preparedness of your recent library hires in the following cataloging and metadata competencies, philosophies, principles and practices: Java and PERL Script Applications? Broken Out by Type of College

Type of College	Not Prepared at All	Minimally Prepared	Prepared	Well Prepared
Community College	33.33%	16.67%	50.00%	0.00%
4-Year Degree Granting College	77.78%	16.67%	5.56%	0.00%
MA or PHD Level Carnegie Class Institution	62.50%	25.00%	12.50%	0.00%
Level 1 or Level 2 Carnegie Class Research University	61.54%	30.77%	0.00%	7.69%

Table 6.16: Please categorize the preparedness of your recent library hires in the following cataloging and metadata competencies, philosophies, principles and practices: Java and PERL Script Applications? Broken Out by Public or Private Status

Public or Private Status	Not Prepared at All	Minimally Prepared	Prepared	Well Prepared
Public	67.86%	17.86%	10.71%	3.57%
Private	58.82%	29.41%	11.76%	0.00%

Table 6.17: Please categorize the preparedness of your recent library hires in the following cataloging and metadata competencies, philosophies, principles and practices: Cataloging Rules and Tools (including Descriptive Cataloging)

	Not Prepared at All	Minimally Prepared	Prepared	Well Prepared
Entire Sample	18.00%	46.00%	18.00%	18.00%

Table 6.18: Please categorize the preparedness of your recent library hires in the following cataloging and metadata competencies, philosophies, principles and practices: Cataloging Rules and Tools (including Descriptive Cataloging)? Broken Out by FTE Student Enrollment

Student Enrollment	Not Prepared at All	Minimally Prepared	Prepared	Well Prepared
Less than 2,000	11.11%	44.44%	22.22%	22.22%
2,000 to 5,000	46.15%	53.85%	0.00%	0.00%
5,000 to 10,000	0.00%	38.46%	38.46%	23.08%
Over 10,000	13.33%	46.67%	13.33%	26.67%

Table 6.19: Please categorize the preparedness of your recent library hires in the following cataloging and metadata competencies, philosophies, principles and practices: Cataloging Rules and Tools (including Descriptive Cataloging)? Broken Out by Type of College

Type of College	Not Prepared at All	Minimally Prepared	Prepared	Well Prepared
Community College	0.00%	100.00%	0.00%	0.00%
4-Year Degree Granting College	19.05%	47.62%	19.05%	14.29%
MA or PHD Level Carnegie Class Institution	40.00%	20.00%	20.00%	20.00%
Level 1 or Level 2 Carnegie Class Research University	7.69%	38.46%	23.08%	30.77%

Table 6.20: Please categorize the preparedness of your recent library hires in the following cataloging and metadata competencies, philosophies, principles and practices: Cataloging Rules and Tools (including Descriptive Cataloging)? Broken Out by Public or Private Status

Public or Private Status	Not Prepared at All	Minimally Prepared	Prepared	Well Prepared
Public	9.68%	54.84%	16.13%	19.35%
Private	31.58%	31.58%	21.05%	15.79%

Table 6.21: Please categorize the preparedness of your recent library hires in the following cataloging and metadata competencies, philosophies, principles and practices: Information Technology and Social Behavior in the Organizational Context?

	Not Prepared at All	Minimally Prepared	Prepared	Well Prepared
Entire Sample	23.40%	31.91%	36.17%	8.51%

Table 6.22: Please categorize the preparedness of your recent library hires in the following cataloging and metadata competencies, philosophies, principles and practices: Information Technology and Social Behavior in the Organizational Context? Broken Out by FTE Student Enrollment

Student Enrollment	Not Prepared at All	Minimally Prepared	Prepared	Well Prepared
Less than 2,000	0.00%	62.50%	25.00%	12.50%
2,000 to 5,000	50.00%	8.33%	41.67%	0.00%
5,000 to 10,000	15.38%	46.15%	30.77%	7.69%
Over 10,000	21.43%	21.43%	42.86%	14.29%

Table 6.23: Please categorize the preparedness of your recent library hires in the following cataloging and metadata competencies, philosophies, principles and practices: Information Technology and Social Behavior in the Organizational Context? Broken Out by Type of College

Type of College	Not Prepared at All	Minimally Prepared	Prepared	Well Prepared
Community College	0.00%	33.33%	66.67%	0.00%
4-Year Degree Granting College	36.84%	36.84%	21.05%	5.26%
MA or PHD Level Carnegie Class Institution	22.22%	22.22%	33.33%	22.22%
Level 1 or Level 2 Carnegie Class Research University	15.38%	30.77%	46.15%	7.69%

Table 6.24:   Please categorize the preparedness of your recent library hires in the following cataloging and metadata competencies, philosophies, principles and practices: Information Technology and Social Behavior in the Organizational Context? Broken Out by Public or Private Status

Public or Private Status	Not Prepared at All	Minimally Prepared	Prepared	Well Prepared
Public	16.67%	33.33%	36.67%	13.33%
Private	35.29%	29.41%	35.29%	0.00%

Table 6.25:   Please categorize the preparedness of your recent library hires in the following cataloging and metadata competencies, philosophies, principles and practices: Metadata standards for Digital Resources (Dublin Core, MODS, VRA, Open Archives Initiative, etc.)?

	Not Prepared at All	Minimally Prepared	Prepared	Well Prepared
Entire Sample	40.00%	42.22%	17.78%	0.00%

Table 6.26:   Please categorize the preparedness of your recent library hires in the following cataloging and metadata competencies, philosophies, principles and practices: Metadata standards for Digital Resources (Dublin Core, MODS, VRA, Open Archives Initiative, etc.)? Broken Out by FTE Student Enrollment

Student Enrollment	Not Prepared at All	Minimally Prepared	Prepared	Well Prepared
Less than 2,000	33.33%	33.33%	33.33%	0.00%
2,000 to 5,000	75.00%	25.00%	0.00%	0.00%
5,000 to 10,000	16.67%	66.67%	16.67%	0.00%
Over 10,000	33.33%	41.67%	25.00%	0.00%

Table 6.27:   Please categorize the preparedness of your recent library hires in the following cataloging and metadata competencies, philosophies, principles and practices: Metadata standards for Digital Resources (Dublin Core, MODS, VRA, Open Archives Initiative, etc.)? Broken Out by Type of College

Type of College	Not Prepared at All	Minimally Prepared	Prepared	Well Prepared
Community College	60.00%	20.00%	20.00%	0.00%
4-Year Degree Granting College	52.63%	31.58%	15.79%	0.00%
MA or PHD Level Carnegie Class Institution	22.22%	55.56%	22.22%	0.00%
Level 1 or Level 2 Carnegie Class Research University	25.00%	58.33%	16.67%	0.00%

Table 6.28:   Please categorize the preparedness of your recent library hires in the following cataloging and metadata competencies, philosophies, principles and practices: Metadata standards for Digital Resources (Dublin Core, MODS, VRA, Open Archives Initiative, etc.) Broken Out by Public or Private Status

Public or Private Status	Not Prepared at All	Minimally Prepared	Prepared	Well Prepared
Public	37.04%	44.44%	18.52%	0.00%
Private	44.44%	38.89%	16.67%	0.00%

Table 6.29:   Please categorize the preparedness of your recent library hires in the following cataloging and metadata competencies, philosophies, principles and practices: Abstracting and Indexing?

	Not Prepared at All	Minimally Prepared	Prepared	Well Prepared
Entire Sample	48.89%	35.56%	15.56%	0.00%

Table 6.30:   Please categorize the preparedness of your recent library hires in the following cataloging and metadata competencies, philosophies, principles and practices: Abstracting and Indexing? Broken Out by FTE Student Enrollment

Student Enrollment	Not Prepared at All	Minimally Prepared	Prepared	Well Prepared
Less than 2,000	55.56%	22.22%	22.22%	0.00%
2,000 to 5,000	83.33%	8.33%	8.33%	0.00%
5,000 to 10,000	33.33%	50.00%	16.67%	0.00%
Over 10,000	25.00%	58.33%	16.67%	0.00%

Table 6.31:   Please categorize the preparedness of your recent library hires in the following cataloging and metadata competencies, philosophies, principles and practices: Abstracting and Indexing? Broken Out by Type of College

Type of College	Not Prepared at All	Minimally Prepared	Prepared	Well Prepared
Community College	66.67%	33.33%	0.00%	0.00%
4-Year Degree Granting College	52.63%	31.58%	15.79%	0.00%
MA or PHD Level Carnegie Class Institution	55.56%	44.44%	0.00%	0.00%
Level 1 or Level 2 Carnegie Class Research University	27.27%	36.36%	36.36%	0.00%

Table 6.32:   Please categorize the preparedness of your recent library hires in the following cataloging and metadata competencies, philosophies, principles and practices: Abstracting and Indexing? Broken Out by Public or Private Status

Public or Private Status	Not Prepared at All	Minimally Prepared	Prepared	Well Prepared
Public	44.44%	44.44%	11.11%	0.00%
Private	55.56%	22.22%	22.22%	0.00%

Table 6.33:   Please categorize the preparedness of your recent library hires in the following cataloging and metadata competencies, philosophies, principles and practices: Electronic delivery of Services?

	Not Prepared at All	Minimally Prepared	Prepared	Well Prepared
Entire Sample	28.26%	41.30%	28.26%	2.17%

Table 6.34:   Please categorize the preparedness of your recent library hires in the following cataloging and metadata competencies, philosophies, principles and practices: Electronic delivery of Services? Broken Out by FTE Student Enrollment

Student Enrollment	Not Prepared at All	Minimally Prepared	Prepared	Well Prepared
Less than 2,000	25.00%	50.00%	25.00%	0.00%
2,000 to 5,000	46.15%	23.08%	30.77%	0.00%
5,000 to 10,000	8.33%	66.67%	25.00%	0.00%
Over 10,000	30.77%	30.77%	30.77%	7.69%

Table 6.35: Please categorize the preparedness of your recent library hires in the following cataloging and metadata competencies, philosophies, principles and practices: Electronic delivery of Services? Broken Out by Type of College

Type of College	Not Prepared at All	Minimally Prepared	Prepared	Well Prepared
Community College	16.67%	50.00%	33.33%	0.00%
4-Year Degree Granting College	47.37%	26.32%	26.32%	0.00%
MA or PHD Level Carnegie Class Institution	22.22%	66.67%	0.00%	11.11%
Level 1 or Level 2 Carnegie Class Research University	8.33%	41.67%	50.00%	0.00%

Table 6.36: Please categorize the preparedness of your recent library hires in the following cataloging and metadata competencies, philosophies, principles and practices: Electronic delivery of Services? Broken Out by Public or Private Status

Public or Private Status	Not Prepared at All	Minimally Prepared	Prepared	Well Prepared
Public	21.43%	50.00%	28.57%	0.00%
Private	38.89%	27.78%	27.78%	5.56%

Table 6.37: Please categorize the preparedness of your recent library hires in the following cataloging and metadata competencies, philosophies, principles and practices: Technical Services in Libraries?

	Not Prepared at All	Minimally Prepared	Prepared	Well Prepared
Entire Sample	22.45%	42.86%	20.41%	14.29%

Table 6.38: Please categorize the preparedness of your recent library hires in the following cataloging and metadata competencies, philosophies, principles and practices: Technical Services in Libraries? Broken Out by FTE Student Enrollment

Student Enrollment	Not Prepared at All	Minimally Prepared	Prepared	Well Prepared
Less than 2,000	33.33%	33.33%	11.11%	22.22%
2,000 to 5,000	46.15%	38.46%	0.00%	15.38%
5,000 to 10,000	0.00%	57.14%	35.71%	7.14%
Over 10,000	15.38%	38.46%	30.77%	15.38%

Table 6.39:   Please categorize the preparedness of your recent library hires in the following cataloging and metadata competencies, philosophies, principles and practices: Technical Services in Libraries? Broken Out by Type of College

Type of College	Not Prepared at All	Minimally Prepared	Prepared	Well Prepared
Community College	28.57%	42.86%	0.00%	28.57%
4-Year Degree Granting College	23.81%	57.14%	4.76%	14.29%
MA or PHD Level Carnegie Class Institution	33.33%	33.33%	33.33%	0.00%
Level 1 or Level 2 Carnegie Class Research University	8.33%	25.00%	50.00%	16.67%

Table 6.40:   Please categorize the preparedness of your recent library hires in the following cataloging and metadata competencies, philosophies, principles and practices: Technical Services in Libraries? Broken Out by Public or Private Status

Public or Private Status	Not Prepared at All	Minimally Prepared	Prepared	Well Prepared
Public	16.67%	46.67%	20.00%	16.67%
Private	31.58%	36.84%	21.05%	10.53%

Table 6.41:   Please categorize the preparedness of your recent library hires in the following cataloging and metadata competencies, philosophies, principles and practices: Web and Local Network System Administration and Management?

	Not Prepared at All	Minimally Prepared	Prepared	Well Prepared
Entire Sample	40.43%	34.04%	25.53%	0.00%

Table 6.42: Please categorize the preparedness of your recent library hires in the following cataloging and metadata competencies, philosophies, principles and practices: Web and Local Network System Administration and Management? Broken Out by FTE Student Enrollment

Student Enrollment	Not Prepared at All	Minimally Prepared	Prepared	Well Prepared
Less than 2,000	37.50%	25.00%	37.50%	0.00%
2,000 to 5,000	69.23%	7.69%	23.08%	0.00%
5,000 to 10,000	25.00%	41.67%	33.33%	0.00%
Over 10,000	28.57%	57.14%	14.29%	0.00%

Table 6.43: Please categorize the preparedness of your recent library hires in the following cataloging and metadata competencies, philosophies, principles and practices: Web and Local Network System Administration and Management? Broken Out by Type of College

Type of College	Not Prepared at All	Minimally Prepared	Prepared	Well Prepared
Community College	50.00%	0.00%	50.00%	0.00%
4-Year Degree Granting College	57.89%	21.05%	21.05%	0.00%
MA or PHD Level Carnegie Class Institution	33.33%	55.56%	11.11%	0.00%
Level 1 or Level 2 Carnegie Class Research University	15.38%	53.85%	30.77%	0.00%

Table 6.44: Please categorize the preparedness of your recent library hires in the following cataloging and metadata competencies, philosophies, principles and practices: Web and Local Network System Administration and Management? Broken Out by Public or Private Status

Public or Private Status	Not Prepared at All	Minimally Prepared	Prepared	Well Prepared
Public	37.93%	34.48%	27.59%	0.00%
Private	44.44%	33.33%	22.22%	0.00%

Table 6.45: Please categorize the preparedness of your recent library hires in the following cataloging and metadata competencies, philosophies, principles and practices: Cataloging Formats - Books?

	Not Prepared at All	Minimally Prepared	Prepared	Well Prepared
Entire Sample	14.00%	48.00%	22.00%	16.00%

Table 6.46: Please categorize the preparedness of your recent library hires in the following cataloging and metadata competencies, philosophies, principles and practices: Cataloging Formats - Books? Broken Out by FTE Student Enrollment

Student Enrollment	Not Prepared at All	Minimally Prepared	Prepared	Well Prepared
Less than 2,000	11.11%	44.44%	33.33%	11.11%
2,000 to 5,000	46.15%	38.46%	7.69%	7.69%
5,000 to 10,000	0.00%	57.14%	21.43%	21.43%
Over 10,000	0.00%	50.00%	28.57%	21.43%

Table 6.47: Please categorize the preparedness of your recent library hires in the following cataloging and metadata competencies, philosophies, principles and practices: Cataloging Formats - Books? Broken Out by Type of College

Type of College	Not Prepared at All	Minimally Prepared	Prepared	Well Prepared
Community College	0.00%	71.43%	14.29%	14.29%
4-Year Degree Granting College	19.05%	52.38%	14.29%	14.29%
MA or PHD Level Carnegie Class Institution	33.33%	22.22%	44.44%	0.00%
Level 1 or Level 2 Carnegie Class Research University	0.00%	46.15%	23.08%	30.77%

Table 6.48: Please categorize the preparedness of your recent library hires in the following cataloging and metadata competencies, philosophies, principles and practices: Cataloging Formats - Books? Broken Out by Public or Private Status

Public or Private Status	Not Prepared at All	Minimally Prepared	Prepared	Well Prepared
Public	6.45%	54.84%	22.58%	16.13%
Private	26.32%	36.84%	21.05%	15.79%

Table 6.49: Please categorize the preparedness of your recent library hires in the following cataloging and metadata competencies, philosophies, principles and practices: Cataloging Formats - Non Books, Digital Resources?

	Not Prepared at All	Minimally Prepared	Prepared	Well Prepared
Entire Sample	32.65%	44.90%	16.33%	6.12%

Table 6.50:   Please categorize the preparedness of your recent library hires in the following cataloging and metadata competencies, philosophies, principles and practices: Cataloging Formats - Non Books, Digital Resources? Broken Out by FTE Student Enrollment

Student Enrollment	Not Prepared at All	Minimally Prepared	Prepared	Well Prepared
Less than 2,000	25.00%	50.00%	25.00%	0.00%
2,000 to 5,000	61.54%	30.77%	7.69%	0.00%
5,000 to 10,000	14.29%	50.00%	21.43%	14.29%
Over 10,000	28.57%	50.00%	14.29%	7.14%

Table 6.51:   Please categorize the preparedness of your recent library hires in the following cataloging and metadata competencies, philosophies, principles and practices: Cataloging Formats - Non Books, Digital Resources? Broken Out by Type of College

Type of College	Not Prepared at All	Minimally Prepared	Prepared	Well Prepared
Community College	0.00%	85.71%	14.29%	0.00%
4-Year Degree Granting College	40.00%	45.00%	15.00%	0.00%
MA or PHD Level Carnegie Class Institution	33.33%	44.44%	22.22%	0.00%
Level 1 or Level 2 Carnegie Class Research University	38.46%	23.08%	15.38%	23.08%

Table 6.52:   Please categorize the preparedness of your recent library hires in the following cataloging and metadata competencies, philosophies, principles and practices: Cataloging Formats - Non Books, Digital Resources? Broken Out by Public or Private Status

Public or Private Status	Not Prepared at All	Minimally Prepared	Prepared	Well Prepared
Public	32.26%	45.16%	19.35%	3.23%
Private	33.33%	44.44%	11.11%	11.11%

Table 6.53:   Please categorize the preparedness of your recent library hires in the following cataloging and metadata competencies, philosophies, principles and practices: Cataloging Formats - Continuing and Integrating Resources?

	Not Prepared at All	Minimally Prepared	Prepared	Well Prepared
Entire Sample	47.92%	27.08%	16.67%	8.33%

Table 6.54: Please categorize the preparedness of your recent library hires in the following cataloging and metadata competencies, philosophies, principles and practices: Cataloging Formats - Continuing and Integrating Resources? Broken Out by FTE Student Enrollment

Student Enrollment	Not Prepared at All	Minimally Prepared	Prepared	Well Prepared
Less than 2,000	44.44%	33.33%	22.22%	0.00%
2,000 to 5,000	75.00%	25.00%	0.00%	0.00%
5,000 to 10,000	30.77%	23.08%	30.77%	15.38%
Over 10,000	42.86%	28.57%	14.29%	14.29%

Table 6.55: Please categorize the preparedness of your recent library hires in the following cataloging and metadata competencies, philosophies, principles and practices: Cataloging Formats - Continuing and Integrating Resources? Broken Out by Type of College

Type of College	Not Prepared at All	Minimally Prepared	Prepared	Well Prepared
Community College	28.57%	71.43%	0.00%	0.00%
4-Year Degree Granting College	57.89%	21.05%	21.05%	0.00%
MA or PHD Level Carnegie Class Institution	44.44%	22.22%	22.22%	11.11%
Level 1 or Level 2 Carnegie Class Research University	46.15%	15.38%	15.38%	23.08%

Table 6.56: Please categorize the preparedness of your recent library hires in the following cataloging and metadata competencies, philosophies, principles and practices: Cataloging Formats - Continuing and Integrating Resources? Broken Out by Public or Private Status

Public or Private Status	Not Prepared at All	Minimally Prepared	Prepared	Well Prepared
Public	50.00%	26.67%	16.67%	6.67%
Private	44.44%	27.78%	16.67%	11.11%

Table 6.57: Please categorize the preparedness of your recent library hires in the following cataloging and metadata competencies, philosophies, principles and practices: Cataloging Special Materials – Law?

	Not Prepared at All	Minimally Prepared	Prepared	Well Prepared
Entire Sample	65.22%	23.91%	6.52%	4.35%

Table 6.58:   Please categorize the preparedness of your recent library hires in the following cataloging and metadata competencies, philosophies, principles and practices: Cataloging Special Materials - Law? Broken Out by FTE Student Enrollment

Student Enrollment	Not Prepared at All	Minimally Prepared	Prepared	Well Prepared
Less than 2,000	55.56%	33.33%	11.11%	0.00%
2,000 to 5,000	100.00%	0.00%	0.00%	0.00%
5,000 to 10,000	33.33%	41.67%	8.33%	16.67%
Over 10,000	71.43%	21.43%	7.14%	0.00%

Table 6.59:   Please categorize the preparedness of your recent library hires in the following cataloging and metadata competencies, philosophies, principles and practices: Cataloging Special Materials - Law? Broken Out by Type of College

Type of College	Not Prepared at All	Minimally Prepared	Prepared	Well Prepared
Community College	50.00%	50.00%	0.00%	0.00%
4-Year Degree Granting College	77.78%	16.67%	5.56%	0.00%
MA or PHD Level Carnegie Class Institution	55.56%	33.33%	11.11%	0.00%
Level 1 or Level 2 Carnegie Class Research University	61.54%	15.38%	7.69%	15.38%

Table 6.60:   Please categorize the preparedness of your recent library hires in the following cataloging and metadata competencies, philosophies, principles and practices: Cataloging Special Materials - Law? Broken Out by Public or Private Status

Public or Private Status	Not Prepared at All	Minimally Prepared	Prepared	Well Prepared
Public	68.97%	20.69%	10.34%	0.00%
Private	58.82%	29.41%	0.00%	11.76%

Table 6.61:   Please categorize the preparedness of your recent library hires in the following cataloging and metadata competencies, philosophies, principles and practices: Cataloging Special Materials – Music?

	Not Prepared at All	Minimally Prepared	Prepared	Well Prepared
Entire Sample	60.87%	19.57%	15.22%	4.35%

Table 6.62:   Please categorize the preparedness of your recent library hires in the following cataloging and metadata competencies, philosophies, principles and practices: Cataloging Special Materials - Music? Broken Out by FTE Student Enrollment

Student Enrollment	Not Prepared at All	Minimally Prepared	Prepared	Well Prepared
Less than 2,000	55.56%	33.33%	11.11%	0.00%
2,000 to 5,000	81.82%	9.09%	9.09%	0.00%
5,000 to 10,000	25.00%	41.67%	16.67%	16.67%
Over 10,000	78.57%	0.00%	21.43%	0.00%

Table 6.63:   Please categorize the preparedness of your recent library hires in the following cataloging and metadata competencies, philosophies, principles and practices: Cataloging Special Materials - Music? Broken Out by Type of College

Type of College	Not Prepared at All	Minimally Prepared	Prepared	Well Prepared
Community College	33.33%	50.00%	16.67%	0.00%
4-Year Degree Granting College	72.22%	16.67%	5.56%	5.56%
MA or PHD Level Carnegie Class Institution	66.67%	22.22%	11.11%	0.00%
Level 1 or Level 2 Carnegie Class Research University	53.85%	7.69%	30.77%	7.69%

Table 6.64:   Please categorize the preparedness of your recent library hires in the following cataloging and metadata competencies, philosophies, principles and practices: Cataloging Special Materials - Music? Broken Out by Public or Private Status

Public or Private Status	Not Prepared at All	Minimally Prepared	Prepared	Well Prepared
Public	58.62%	17.24%	20.69%	3.45%
Private	64.71%	23.53%	5.88%	5.88%

Table 6.65:   Please categorize the preparedness of your recent library hires in the following cataloging and metadata competencies, philosophies, principles and practices: Cataloging Special Materials - Archives and Rare Materials?

	Not Prepared at All	Minimally Prepared	Prepared	Well Prepared
Entire Sample	53.19%	29.79%	14.89%	2.13%

Table 6.66: Please categorize the preparedness of your recent library hires in the following cataloging and metadata competencies, philosophies, principles and practices: Cataloging Special Materials - Archives and Rare Materials? Broken Out by FTE Student Enrollment

Student Enrollment	Not Prepared at All	Minimally Prepared	Prepared	Well Prepared
Less than 2,000	55.56%	33.33%	11.11%	0.00%
2,000 to 5,000	75.00%	25.00%	0.00%	0.00%
5,000 to 10,000	25.00%	33.33%	33.33%	8.33%
Over 10,000	57.14%	28.57%	14.29%	0.00%

Table 6.67: Please categorize the preparedness of your recent library hires in the following cataloging and metadata competencies, philosophies, principles and practices: Cataloging Special Materials - Archives and Rare Materials? Broken Out by Type of College

Type of College	Not Prepared at All	Minimally Prepared	Prepared	Well Prepared
Community College	66.67%	33.33%	0.00%	0.00%
4-Year Degree Granting College	57.89%	31.58%	10.53%	0.00%
MA or PHD Level Carnegie Class Institution	55.56%	22.22%	22.22%	0.00%
Level 1 or Level 2 Carnegie Class Research University	38.46%	30.77%	23.08%	7.69%

Table 6.68: Please categorize the preparedness of your recent library hires in the following cataloging and metadata competencies, philosophies, principles and practices: Cataloging Special Materials - Archives and Rare Materials? Broken Out by Public or Private Status

Public or Private Status	Not Prepared at All	Minimally Prepared	Prepared	Well Prepared
Public	51.72%	31.03%	17.24%	0.00%
Private	55.56%	27.78%	11.11%	5.56%

Table 6.69: Please categorize the preparedness of your recent library hires in the following cataloging and metadata competencies, philosophies, principles and practices: XML and/or XSLT?

	Not Prepared at All	Minimally Prepared	Prepared	Well Prepared
Entire Sample	60.42%	25.00%	12.50%	2.08%

Table 6.70: **Please categorize the preparedness of your recent library hires in the following cataloging and metadata competencies, philosophies, principles and practices: XML and/or XSLT? Broken Out by FTE Student Enrollment**

Student Enrollment	Not Prepared at All	Minimally Prepared	Prepared	Well Prepared
Less than 2,000	66.67%	0.00%	33.33%	0.00%
2,000 to 5,000	75.00%	16.67%	8.33%	0.00%
5,000 to 10,000	46.15%	46.15%	7.69%	0.00%
Over 10,000	57.14%	28.57%	7.14%	7.14%

Table 6.71: **Please categorize the preparedness of your recent library hires in the following cataloging and metadata competencies, philosophies, principles and practices: XML and/or XSLT? Broken Out by Type of College**

Type of College	Not Prepared at All	Minimally Prepared	Prepared	Well Prepared
Community College	57.14%	14.29%	28.57%	0.00%
4-Year Degree Granting College	84.21%	5.26%	10.53%	0.00%
MA or PHD Level Carnegie Class Institution	33.33%	44.44%	22.22%	0.00%
Level 1 or Level 2 Carnegie Class Research University	46.15%	46.15%	0.00%	7.69%

Table 6.72: **Please categorize the preparedness of your recent library hires in the following cataloging and metadata competencies, philosophies, principles and practices: XML and/or XSLT? Broken Out by Public or Private Status**

Public or Private Status	Not Prepared at All	Minimally Prepared	Prepared	Well Prepared
Public	56.67%	30.00%	10.00%	3.33%
Private	66.67%	16.67%	16.67%	0.00%

Table 6.73: **Please categorize the preparedness of your recent library hires in the following cataloging and metadata competencies, philosophies, principles and practices: Economics and Metrics of Information?**

	Not Prepared at All	Minimally Prepared	Prepared	Well Prepared
Entire Sample	57.78%	35.56%	6.67%	0.00%

Table 6.74:   Please categorize the preparedness of your recent library hires in the following cataloging and metadata competencies, philosophies, principles and practices: Economics and Metrics of Information? Broken Out by FTE Student Enrollment

Student Enrollment	Not Prepared at All	Minimally Prepared	Prepared	Well Prepared
Less than 2,000	55.56%	33.33%	11.11%	0.00%
2,000 to 5,000	81.82%	18.18%	0.00%	0.00%
5,000 to 10,000	36.36%	54.55%	9.09%	0.00%
Over 10,000	57.14%	35.71%	7.14%	0.00%

Table 6.75:   Please categorize the preparedness of your recent library hires in the following cataloging and metadata competencies, philosophies, principles and practices: Economics and Metrics of Information? Broken Out by Type of College

Type of College	Not Prepared at All	Minimally Prepared	Prepared	Well Prepared
Community College	40.00%	40.00%	20.00%	0.00%
4-Year Degree Granting College	77.78%	22.22%	0.00%	0.00%
MA or PHD Level Carnegie Class Institution	33.33%	55.56%	11.11%	0.00%
Level 1 or Level 2 Carnegie Class Research University	53.85%	38.46%	7.69%	0.00%

Table 6.76:   Please categorize the preparedness of your recent library hires in the following cataloging and metadata competencies, philosophies, principles and practices: Economics and Metrics of Information? Broken Out by Public or Private Status

Public or Private Status	Not Prepared at All	Minimally Prepared	Prepared	Well Prepared
Public	57.14%	35.71%	7.14%	0.00%
Private	58.82%	35.29%	5.88%	0.00%

Table 6.77:   Please categorize the preparedness of your recent library hires in the following cataloging and metadata competencies, philosophies, principles and practices: Discovery Tools and Applications?

	Not Prepared at All	Minimally Prepared	Prepared	Well Prepared
Entire Sample	27.66%	42.55%	23.40%	6.38%

Table 6.78:   Please categorize the preparedness of your recent library hires in the following cataloging and metadata competencies, philosophies, principles and practices: Discovery Tools and Applications? Broken Out by FTE Student Enrollment

Student Enrollment	Not Prepared at All	Minimally Prepared	Prepared	Well Prepared
Less than 2,000	11.11%	55.56%	33.33%	0.00%
2,000 to 5,000	38.46%	46.15%	15.38%	0.00%
5,000 to 10,000	27.27%	45.45%	27.27%	0.00%
Over 10,000	28.57%	28.57%	21.43%	21.43%

Table 6.79:   Please categorize the preparedness of your recent library hires in the following cataloging and metadata competencies, philosophies, principles and practices: Discovery Tools and Applications? Broken Out by Type of College

Type of College	Not Prepared at All	Minimally Prepared	Prepared	Well Prepared
Community College	40.00%	60.00%	0.00%	0.00%
4-Year Degree Granting College	30.00%	45.00%	25.00%	0.00%
MA or PHD Level Carnegie Class Institution	22.22%	44.44%	11.11%	22.22%
Level 1 or Level 2 Carnegie Class Research University	23.08%	30.77%	38.46%	7.69%

Table 6.80:   Please categorize the preparedness of your recent library hires in the following cataloging and metadata competencies, philosophies, principles and practices: Discovery Tools and Applications? Broken Out by Public or Private Status

Public or Private Status	Not Prepared at All	Minimally Prepared	Prepared	Well Prepared
Public	25.00%	50.00%	17.86%	7.14%
Private	31.58%	31.58%	31.58%	5.26%

Table 6.81:   Please categorize the preparedness of your recent library hires in the following cataloging and metadata competencies, philosophies, principles and practices: Authority Control?

	Not Prepared at All	Minimally Prepared	Prepared	Well Prepared
Entire Sample	33.33%	45.83%	14.58%	6.25%

Table 6.82: Please categorize the preparedness of your recent library hires in the following cataloging and metadata competencies, philosophies, principles and practices: Authority Control? Broken Out by FTE Student Enrollment

Student Enrollment	Not Prepared at All	Minimally Prepared	Prepared	Well Prepared
Less than 2,000	55.56%	11.11%	33.33%	0.00%
2,000 to 5,000	63.64%	36.36%	0.00%	0.00%
5,000 to 10,000	7.14%	64.29%	14.29%	14.29%
Over 10,000	21.43%	57.14%	14.29%	7.14%

Table 6.83: Please categorize the preparedness of your recent library hires in the following cataloging and metadata competencies, philosophies, principles and practices: Authority Control? Broken Out by Type of College

Type of College	Not Prepared at All	Minimally Prepared	Prepared	Well Prepared
Community College	42.86%	57.14%	0.00%	0.00%
4-Year Degree Granting College	36.84%	47.37%	10.53%	5.26%
MA or PHD Level Carnegie Class Institution	55.56%	11.11%	33.33%	0.00%
Level 1 or Level 2 Carnegie Class Research University	7.69%	61.54%	15.38%	15.38%

Table 6.84: Please categorize the preparedness of your recent library hires in the following cataloging and metadata competencies, philosophies, principles and practices: Authority Control? Broken Out by Public or Private Status

Public or Private Status	Not Prepared at All	Minimally Prepared	Prepared	Well Prepared
Public	23.33%	56.67%	13.33%	6.67%
Private	50.00%	27.78%	16.67%	5.56%

Table 6.85: Please categorize the preparedness of your recent library hires in the following cataloging and metadata competencies, philosophies, principles and practices: Web Usability, User Research, and Human Interface Design?

	Not Prepared at All	Minimally Prepared	Prepared	Well Prepared
Entire Sample	22.92%	33.33%	39.58%	4.17%

Table 6.86:   Please categorize the preparedness of your recent library hires in the following cataloging and metadata competencies, philosophies, principles and practices: Web Usability, User Research, and Human Interface Design? Broken Out by FTE Student Enrollment

Student Enrollment	Not Prepared at All	Minimally Prepared	Prepared	Well Prepared
Less than 2,000	22.22%	22.22%	55.56%	0.00%
2,000 to 5,000	33.33%	41.67%	25.00%	0.00%
5,000 to 10,000	15.38%	38.46%	46.15%	0.00%
Over 10,000	21.43%	28.57%	35.71%	14.29%

Table 6.87:   Please categorize the preparedness of your recent library hires in the following cataloging and metadata competencies, philosophies, principles and practices: Web Usability, User Research, and Human Interface Design? Broken Out by Type of College

Type of College	Not Prepared at All	Minimally Prepared	Prepared	Well Prepared
Community College	0.00%	42.86%	57.14%	0.00%
4-Year Degree Granting College	36.84%	26.32%	36.84%	0.00%
MA or PHD Level Carnegie Class Institution	22.22%	22.22%	44.44%	11.11%
Level 1 or Level 2 Carnegie Class Research University	15.38%	46.15%	30.77%	7.69%

Table 6.88:   Please categorize the preparedness of your recent library hires in the following cataloging and metadata competencies, philosophies, principles and practices: Web Usability, User Research, and Human Interface Design? Broken Out by Public or Private Status

Public or Private Status	Not Prepared at All	Minimally Prepared	Prepared	Well Prepared
Public	13.33%	36.67%	46.67%	3.33%
Private	38.89%	27.78%	27.78%	5.56%

Table 6.89:   Please categorize the preparedness of your recent library hires in the following cataloging and metadata competencies, philosophies, principles and practices: International MARC Bibliographic, Authority and Holdings Standards?

	Not Prepared at All	Minimally Prepared	Prepared	Well Prepared
Entire Sample	24.49%	42.86%	18.37%	14.29%

Table 6.90: Please categorize the preparedness of your recent library hires in the following cataloging and metadata competencies, philosophies, principles and practices: International MARC Bibliographic, Authority and Holdings Standards? Broken Out by FTE Student Enrollment

Student Enrollment	Not Prepared at All	Minimally Prepared	Prepared	Well Prepared
Less than 2,000	33.33%	33.33%	22.22%	11.11%
2,000 to 5,000	58.33%	33.33%	0.00%	8.33%
5,000 to 10,000	0.00%	50.00%	28.57%	21.43%
Over 10,000	14.29%	50.00%	21.43%	14.29%

Table 6.91: Please categorize the preparedness of your recent library hires in the following cataloging and metadata competencies, philosophies, principles and practices: International MARC Bibliographic, Authority and Holdings Standards? Broken Out by Type of College

Type of College	Not Prepared at All	Minimally Prepared	Prepared	Well Prepared
Community College	0.00%	85.71%	0.00%	14.29%
4-Year Degree Granting College	35.00%	40.00%	10.00%	15.00%
MA or PHD Level Carnegie Class Institution	44.44%	11.11%	44.44%	0.00%
Level 1 or Level 2 Carnegie Class Research University	7.69%	46.15%	23.08%	23.08%

Table 6.92: Please categorize the preparedness of your recent library hires in the following cataloging and metadata competencies, philosophies, principles and practices: International MARC Bibliographic, Authority and Holdings Standards? Broken Out by Public or Private Status

Public or Private Status	Not Prepared at All	Minimally Prepared	Prepared	Well Prepared
Public	9.68%	58.06%	19.35%	12.90%
Private	50.00%	16.67%	16.67%	16.67%

Table 6.93: Please categorize the preparedness of your recent library hires in the following cataloging and metadata competencies, philosophies, principles and practices: Data Modeling, Warehousing, Mining?

	Not Prepared at All	Minimally Prepared	Prepared	Well Prepared
Entire Sample	51.06%	34.04%	14.89%	0.00%

147

Table 6.94:   Please categorize the preparedness of your recent library hires in the following cataloging and metadata competencies, philosophies, principles and practices: Data Modeling, Warehousing, Mining? Broken Out by FTE Student Enrollment

Student Enrollment	Not Prepared at All	Minimally Prepared	Prepared	Well Prepared
Less than 2,000	55.56%	11.11%	33.33%	0.00%
2,000 to 5,000	66.67%	25.00%	8.33%	0.00%
5,000 to 10,000	16.67%	75.00%	8.33%	0.00%
Over 10,000	64.29%	21.43%	14.29%	0.00%

Table 6.95:   Please categorize the preparedness of your recent library hires in the following cataloging and metadata competencies, philosophies, principles and practices: Data Modeling, Warehousing, Mining? Broken Out by Type of College

Type of College	Not Prepared at All	Minimally Prepared	Prepared	Well Prepared
Community College	33.33%	33.33%	33.33%	0.00%
4-Year Degree Granting College	63.16%	26.32%	10.53%	0.00%
MA or PHD Level Carnegie Class Institution	33.33%	44.44%	22.22%	0.00%
Level 1 or Level 2 Carnegie Class Research University	53.85%	38.46%	7.69%	0.00%

Table 6.96:   Please categorize the preparedness of your recent library hires in the following cataloging and metadata competencies, philosophies, principles and practices: Data Modeling, Warehousing, Mining? Broken Out by Public or Private Status

Public or Private Status	Not Prepared at All	Minimally Prepared	Prepared	Well Prepared
Public	44.83%	41.38%	13.79%	0.00%
Private	61.11%	22.22%	16.67%	0.00%

Table 6.97:   Please categorize the preparedness of your recent library hires in the following cataloging and metadata competencies, philosophies, principles and practices: Information Systems Analysis?

	Not Prepared at All	Minimally Prepared	Prepared	Well Prepared
Entire Sample	42.55%	40.43%	17.02%	0.00%

Table 6.98: Please categorize the preparedness of your recent library hires in the following cataloging and metadata competencies, philosophies, principles and practices: Information Systems Analysis? Broken Out by FTE Student Enrollment

Student Enrollment	Not Prepared at All	Minimally Prepared	Prepared	Well Prepared
Less than 2,000	44.44%	33.33%	22.22%	0.00%
2,000 to 5,000	50.00%	25.00%	25.00%	0.00%
5,000 to 10,000	16.67%	75.00%	8.33%	0.00%
Over 10,000	57.14%	28.57%	14.29%	0.00%

Table 6.99: Please categorize the preparedness of your recent library hires in the following cataloging and metadata competencies, philosophies, principles and practices: Information Systems Analysis? Broken Out by Type of College

Type of College	Not Prepared at All	Minimally Prepared	Prepared	Well Prepared
Community College	33.33%	16.67%	50.00%	0.00%
4-Year Degree Granting College	52.63%	36.84%	10.53%	0.00%
MA or PHD Level Carnegie Class Institution	33.33%	44.44%	22.22%	0.00%
Level 1 or Level 2 Carnegie Class Research University	38.46%	53.85%	7.69%	0.00%

Table 6.100: Please categorize the preparedness of your recent library hires in the following cataloging and metadata competencies, philosophies, principles and practices: Information Systems Analysis? Broken Out by Public or Private Status

Public or Private Status	Not Prepared at All	Minimally Prepared	Prepared	Well Prepared
Public	37.93%	44.83%	17.24%	0.00%
Private	50.00%	33.33%	16.67%	0.00%

Table 6.101: Please categorize the preparedness of your recent library hires in the following cataloging and metadata competencies, philosophies, principles and practices: Programming Languages and Applications?

	Not Prepared at All	Minimally Prepared	Prepared	Well Prepared
Entire Sample	63.83%	21.28%	14.89%	0.00%

Table 6.102: Please categorize the preparedness of your recent library hires in the following cataloging and metadata competencies, philosophies, principles and practices: Programming Languages and Applications? Broken Out by FTE Student Enrollment

Student Enrollment	Not Prepared at All	Minimally Prepared	Prepared	Well Prepared
Less than 2,000	66.67%	11.11%	22.22%	0.00%
2,000 to 5,000	58.33%	33.33%	8.33%	0.00%
5,000 to 10,000	58.33%	25.00%	16.67%	0.00%
Over 10,000	71.43%	14.29%	14.29%	0.00%

Table 6.103: Please categorize the preparedness of your recent library hires in the following cataloging and metadata competencies, philosophies, principles and practices: Programming Languages and Applications? Broken Out by Type of College

Type of College	Not Prepared at All	Minimally Prepared	Prepared	Well Prepared
Community College	50.00%	16.67%	33.33%	0.00%
4-Year Degree Granting College	78.95%	15.79%	5.26%	0.00%
MA or PHD Level Carnegie Class Institution	44.44%	22.22%	33.33%	0.00%
Level 1 or Level 2 Carnegie Class Research University	61.54%	30.77%	7.69%	0.00%

Table 6.104: Please categorize the preparedness of your recent library hires in the following cataloging and metadata competencies, philosophies, principles and practices: Programming Languages and Applications? Broken Out by Public or Private Status

Public or Private Status	Not Prepared at All	Minimally Prepared	Prepared	Well Prepared
Public	58.62%	27.59%	13.79%	0.00%
Private	72.22%	11.11%	16.67%	0.00%

Table 6.105: Please categorize the preparedness of your recent library hires in the following cataloging and metadata competencies, philosophies, principles and practices: Relational Database Design?

	Not Prepared at All	Minimally Prepared	Prepared	Well Prepared
Entire Sample	58.33%	25.00%	16.67%	0.00%

Table 6.106: Please categorize the preparedness of your recent library hires in the following cataloging and metadata competencies, philosophies, principles and practices: Relational Database Design? Broken Out by FTE Student Enrollment

Student Enrollment	Not Prepared at All	Minimally Prepared	Prepared	Well Prepared
Less than 2,000	44.44%	33.33%	22.22%	0.00%
2,000 to 5,000	66.67%	8.33%	25.00%	0.00%
5,000 to 10,000	46.15%	46.15%	7.69%	0.00%
Over 10,000	71.43%	14.29%	14.29%	0.00%

Table 6.107: Please categorize the preparedness of your recent library hires in the following cataloging and metadata competencies, philosophies, principles and practices: Relational Database Design? Broken Out by Type of College

Type of College	Not Prepared at All	Minimally Prepared	Prepared	Well Prepared
Community College	14.29%	28.57%	57.14%	0.00%
4-Year Degree Granting College	63.16%	31.58%	5.26%	0.00%
MA or PHD Level Carnegie Class Institution	55.56%	22.22%	22.22%	0.00%
Level 1 or Level 2 Carnegie Class Research University	76.92%	15.38%	7.69%	0.00%

Table 6.108: Please categorize the preparedness of your recent library hires in the following cataloging and metadata competencies, philosophies, principles and practices: Relational Database Design? Broken Out by Public or Private Status

Public or Private Status	Not Prepared at All	Minimally Prepared	Prepared	Well Prepared
Public	56.67%	23.33%	20.00%	0.00%
Private	61.11%	27.78%	11.11%	0.00%

Table 6.109: Please categorize the preparedness of your recent library hires in the following cataloging and metadata competencies, philosophies, principles and practices: OCLC Systems and Services?

	Not Prepared at All	Minimally Prepared	Prepared	Well Prepared
Entire Sample	25.00%	39.58%	29.17%	6.25%

Table 6.110:   Please categorize the preparedness of your recent library hires in the following cataloging and metadata competencies, philosophies, principles and practices: OCLC Systems and Services? Broken Out by FTE Student Enrollment

Student Enrollment	Not Prepared at All	Minimally Prepared	Prepared	Well Prepared
Less than 2,000	44.44%	22.22%	22.22%	11.11%
2,000 to 5,000	33.33%	50.00%	16.67%	0.00%
5,000 to 10,000	7.69%	46.15%	38.46%	7.69%
Over 10,000	21.43%	35.71%	35.71%	7.14%

Table 6.111:   Please categorize the preparedness of your recent library hires in the following cataloging and metadata competencies, philosophies, principles and practices: OCLC Systems and Services? Broken Out by Type of College

Type of College	Not Prepared at All	Minimally Prepared	Prepared	Well Prepared
Community College	0.00%	50.00%	50.00%	0.00%
4-Year Degree Granting College	35.00%	40.00%	20.00%	5.00%
MA or PHD Level Carnegie Class Institution	33.33%	33.33%	33.33%	0.00%
Level 1 or Level 2 Carnegie Class Research University	15.38%	38.46%	30.77%	15.38%

Table 6.112:   Please categorize the preparedness of your recent library hires in the following cataloging and metadata competencies, philosophies, principles and practices: OCLC Systems and Services? Broken Out by Public or Private Status

Public or Private Status	Not Prepared at All	Minimally Prepared	Prepared	Well Prepared
Public	13.33%	50.00%	33.33%	3.33%
Private	44.44%	22.22%	22.22%	11.11%

Table 6.113:   Please categorize the preparedness of your recent library hires in the following cataloging and metadata competencies, philosophies, principles and practices: Digital Libraries and Collections?

	Not Prepared at All	Minimally Prepared	Prepared	Well Prepared
Entire Sample	25.00%	41.67%	27.08%	6.25%

Table 6.114: Please categorize the preparedness of your recent library hires in the following cataloging and metadata competencies, philosophies, principles and practices: Digital Libraries and Collections? Broken Out by FTE Student Enrollment

Student Enrollment	Not Prepared at All	Minimally Prepared	Prepared	Well Prepared
Less than 2,000	44.44%	11.11%	44.44%	0.00%
2,000 to 5,000	41.67%	33.33%	16.67%	8.33%
5,000 to 10,000	7.69%	46.15%	46.15%	0.00%
Over 10,000	14.29%	64.29%	7.14%	14.29%

Table 6.115: Please categorize the preparedness of your recent library hires in the following cataloging and metadata competencies, philosophies, principles and practices: Digital Libraries and Collections? Broken Out by Type of College

Type of College	Not Prepared at All	Minimally Prepared	Prepared	Well Prepared
Community College	0.00%	14.29%	71.43%	14.29%
4-Year Degree Granting College	36.84%	36.84%	26.32%	0.00%
MA or PHD Level Carnegie Class Institution	33.33%	55.56%	11.11%	0.00%
Level 1 or Level 2 Carnegie Class Research University	15.38%	53.85%	15.38%	15.38%

Table 6.116: Please categorize the preparedness of your recent library hires in the following cataloging and metadata competencies, philosophies, principles and practices: Digital Libraries and Collections? Broken Out by Public or Private Status

Public or Private Status	Not Prepared at All	Minimally Prepared	Prepared	Well Prepared
Public	10.00%	46.67%	33.33%	10.00%
Private	50.00%	33.33%	16.67%	0.00%

Table 6.117: Please categorize the preparedness of your recent library hires in the following cataloging and metadata competencies, philosophies, principles and practices: Practicum: Experiential Learning?

	Not Prepared at All	Minimally Prepared	Prepared	Well Prepared
Entire Sample	21.74%	43.48%	26.09%	8.70%

Table 6.118: Please categorize the preparedness of your recent library hires in the following cataloging and metadata competencies, philosophies, principles and practices: Practicum: Experiential Learning? Broken Out by FTE Student Enrollment

Student Enrollment	Not Prepared at All	Minimally Prepared	Prepared	Well Prepared
Less than 2,000	22.22%	44.44%	33.33%	0.00%
2,000 to 5,000	33.33%	33.33%	25.00%	8.33%
5,000 to 10,000	16.67%	50.00%	16.67%	16.67%
Over 10,000	15.38%	46.15%	30.77%	7.69%

Table 6.119: Please categorize the preparedness of your recent library hires in the following cataloging and metadata competencies, philosophies, principles and practices: Experiential Learning? Broken Out by Type of College

Type of College	Not Prepared at All	Minimally Prepared	Prepared	Well Prepared
Community College	20.00%	40.00%	20.00%	20.00%
4-Year Degree Granting College	20.00%	45.00%	30.00%	5.00%
MA or PHD Level Carnegie Class Institution	22.22%	55.56%	11.11%	11.11%
Level 1 or Level 2 Carnegie Class Research University	25.00%	33.33%	33.33%	8.33%

Table 6.120: Please categorize the preparedness of your recent library hires in the following cataloging and metadata competencies, philosophies, principles and practices: Experiential Learning? Broken Out by Public or Private Status

Public or Private Status	Not Prepared at All	Minimally Prepared	Prepared	Well Prepared
Public	10.71%	50.00%	28.57%	10.71%
Private	38.89%	33.33%	22.22%	5.56%

Table 6.121: Please categorize the preparedness of your recent library hires in the following cataloging and metadata competencies, philosophies, principles and practices: Information Storage, Retrieval, Architecture?

	Not Prepared at All	Minimally Prepared	Prepared	Well Prepared
Entire Sample	30.43%	43.48%	23.91%	2.17%

Table 6.122: Please categorize the preparedness of your recent library hires in the following cataloging and metadata competencies, philosophies, principles and practices: Information Storage, Retrieval, Architecture? Broken Out by FTE Student Enrollment

Student Enrollment	Not Prepared at All	Minimally Prepared	Prepared	Well Prepared
Less than 2,000	44.44%	44.44%	11.11%	0.00%
2,000 to 5,000	41.67%	33.33%	25.00%	0.00%
5,000 to 10,000	18.18%	45.45%	27.27%	9.09%
Over 10,000	21.43%	50.00%	28.57%	0.00%

Table 6.123: Please categorize the preparedness of your recent library hires in the following cataloging and metadata competencies, philosophies, principles and practices: Information Storage, Retrieval, Architecture? Broken Out by Type of College

Type of College	Not Prepared at All	Minimally Prepared	Prepared	Well Prepared
Community College	0.00%	60.00%	40.00%	0.00%
4-Year Degree Granting College	42.11%	47.37%	10.53%	0.00%
MA or PHD Level Carnegie Class Institution	33.33%	33.33%	33.33%	0.00%
Level 1 or Level 2 Carnegie Class Research University	23.08%	38.46%	30.77%	7.69%

Table 6.124: Please categorize the preparedness of your recent library hires in the following cataloging and metadata competencies, philosophies, principles and practices: Information Storage, Retrieval, Architecture? Broken Out by Public or Private Status

Public or Private Status	Not Prepared at All	Minimally Prepared	Prepared	Well Prepared
Public	17.86%	50.00%	32.14%	0.00%
Private	50.00%	33.33%	11.11%	5.56%

Table 6.125: Please categorize the preparedness of your recent library hires in the following cataloging and metadata competencies, philosophies, principles and practices: Social Networking and Information?

	Not Prepared at All	Minimally Prepared	Prepared	Well Prepared
Entire Sample	16.33%	26.53%	44.90%	12.24%

Table 6.126:   Please categorize the preparedness of your recent library hires in the following cataloging and metadata competencies, philosophies, principles and practices: Social Networking and Information? Broken Out by FTE Student Enrollment

Student Enrollment	Not Prepared at All	Minimally Prepared	Prepared	Well Prepared
Less than 2,000	11.11%	44.44%	44.44%	0.00%
2,000 to 5,000	25.00%	25.00%	41.67%	8.33%
5,000 to 10,000	15.38%	23.08%	46.15%	15.38%
Over 10,000	13.33%	20.00%	46.67%	20.00%

Table 6.127:   Please categorize the preparedness of your recent library hires in the following cataloging and metadata competencies, philosophies, principles and practices: Social Networking and Information? Broken Out by Type of College

Type of College	Not Prepared at All	Minimally Prepared	Prepared	Well Prepared
Community College	0.00%	14.29%	57.14%	28.57%
4-Year Degree Granting College	26.32%	42.11%	31.58%	0.00%
MA or PHD Level Carnegie Class Institution	10.00%	40.00%	40.00%	10.00%
Level 1 or Level 2 Carnegie Class Research University	15.38%	0.00%	61.54%	23.08%

Table 6.128:   Please categorize the preparedness of your recent library hires in the following cataloging and metadata competencies, philosophies, principles and practices: Social Networking and Information? Broken Out by Public or Private Status

Public or Private Status	Not Prepared at All	Minimally Prepared	Prepared	Well Prepared
Public	9.68%	19.35%	51.61%	19.35%
Private	27.78%	38.89%	33.33%	0.00%

Table 6.129:   Please categorize the preparedness of your recent library hires in the following cataloging and metadata competencies, philosophies, principles and practices: Electronic Publishing and Scholarly Communication?

	Not Prepared at All	Minimally Prepared	Prepared	Well Prepared
Entire Sample	22.92%	43.75%	31.25%	2.08%

Table 6.130: Please categorize the preparedness of your recent library hires in the following cataloging and metadata competencies, philosophies, principles and practices: Electronic Publishing and Scholarly Communication? Broken Out by FTE Student Enrollment

Student Enrollment	Not Prepared at All	Minimally Prepared	Prepared	Well Prepared
Less than 2,000	33.33%	44.44%	22.22%	0.00%
2,000 to 5,000	41.67%	25.00%	25.00%	8.33%
5,000 to 10,000	7.69%	61.54%	30.77%	0.00%
Over 10,000	14.29%	42.86%	42.86%	0.00%

Table 6.131: Please categorize the preparedness of your recent library hires in the following cataloging and metadata competencies, philosophies, principles and practices: Electronic Publishing and Scholarly Communication? Broken Out by Type of College

Type of College	Not Prepared at All	Minimally Prepared	Prepared	Well Prepared
Community College	0.00%	14.29%	71.43%	14.29%
4-Year Degree Granting College	36.84%	57.89%	5.26%	0.00%
MA or PHD Level Carnegie Class Institution	33.33%	33.33%	33.33%	0.00%
Level 1 or Level 2 Carnegie Class Research University	7.69%	46.15%	46.15%	0.00%

Table 6.132: Please categorize the preparedness of your recent library hires in the following cataloging and metadata competencies, philosophies, principles and practices: Electronic Publishing and Scholarly Communication? Broken Out by Public or Private Status

Public or Private Status	Not Prepared at All	Minimally Prepared	Prepared	Well Prepared
Public	10.00%	40.00%	46.67%	3.33%
Private	44.44%	50.00%	5.56%	0.00%

Table 6.133: Please categorize the preparedness of your recent library hires in the following cataloging and metadata competencies, philosophies, principles and practices: Principles of Historical and Contemporary Bibliographic Control?

	Not Prepared at All	Minimally Prepared	Prepared	Well Prepared
Entire Sample	40.43%	31.91%	17.02%	10.64%

Table 6.134: Please categorize the preparedness of your recent library hires in the following cataloging and metadata competencies, philosophies, principles and practices: Principles of Historical and Contemporary Bibliographic Control? Broken Out by FTE Student Enrollment

Student Enrollment	Not Prepared at All	Minimally Prepared	Prepared	Well Prepared
Less than 2,000	44.44%	22.22%	22.22%	11.11%
2,000 to 5,000	58.33%	25.00%	16.67%	0.00%
5,000 to 10,000	8.33%	66.67%	8.33%	16.67%
Over 10,000	50.00%	14.29%	21.43%	14.29%

Table 6.135: Please categorize the preparedness of your recent library hires in the following cataloging and metadata competencies, philosophies, principles and practices: Principles of Historical and Contemporary Bibliographic Control? Broken Out by Type of College

Type of College	Not Prepared at All	Minimally Prepared	Prepared	Well Prepared
Community College	16.67%	50.00%	33.33%	0.00%
4-Year Degree Granting College	52.63%	26.32%	10.53%	10.53%
MA or PHD Level Carnegie Class Institution	44.44%	33.33%	11.11%	11.11%
Level 1 or Level 2 Carnegie Class Research University	30.77%	30.77%	23.08%	15.38%

Table 6.136: Please categorize the preparedness of your recent library hires in the following cataloging and metadata competencies, philosophies, principles and practices: Principles of Historical and Contemporary Bibliographic Control? Broken Out by Public or Private Status

Public or Private Status	Not Prepared at All	Minimally Prepared	Prepared	Well Prepared
Public	31.03%	37.93%	20.69%	10.34%
Private	55.56%	22.22%	11.11%	11.11%